Copyright © 2020 Tekkan
Artwork Copyright © 2020

All rights reserved.
First Printing, 2020
ISBN 978-1-7343510-7-1

To contact Tekkan please email:
buddhaboy1289@gmail.com

Table of Contents

Everyday Mind XI . . . . Page 1

Everyday Mind XII . . . . Page 102

Everyday Mind XIII . . . . Page 202

Everyday Mind XIV . . . . Page 302

Everyday Mind XV . . . . Page 402

Introduction

I am an ordinary guy living a middle class life. I may imagine what it would be like to put on a wingsuit and jump off a mountain, but my stock-in-trade is the exploration of "everyday mind." I look for transcendent meaning in the ordinary happenings of daily life. I write in the morning everyday, and try to distill experience down to essentials. It is easy to overlook the instant-by-instant process of seeing, thinking, and responding to life — but in reality that is what life is.

The mind is self-interested and driven by powerful emotions. I look around and determine what to do. I judge what's worthy, and establish a list of priorities. My likes and dislikes become signposts, and if I am not careful I find myself repeating a pattern of behavior, and get stuck, narrowly seeing, feeling, experiencing — and then where is novelty?

Spring has sprung but today is chilly. I love watching the seasons change in a succession of little details, because the seasons are so much bigger than what's going on in my mind. There is always a lot going on in nature, and my practice is to open, so that more of reality may penetrate my consciousness.

I practice opening my awareness to the world inside and outside of me. Consciousness is a miracle — but I have to learn how to use the gift of Consciousness. This is what my poetry is about.

How to Read My Poems

I have married the sonnet to the tanka. I tell a story in the sonnet — using three quatrains, separated by line spaces, and a final couplet. The story builds to a conclusion in the couplet. The tanka is a commentary, or a counterpoint, to the sonnet — the combined poems have two endings.

I don't rhyme my sonnets, because I want freer expression. I want to be direct in my meaning — I want people to clearly understand my meaning. The metaphors are inspired by Shakespeare, and the (aimed-for) precision is in imitation of Japanese style. Using the sonnet with the tanka, I am mixing the sensibility of the Occident and the Orient — which I have done by living in England, Japan, and America.

I don't punctuate much in my poetry. I want the words themselves to do the work. There is logic between words, and the forms provide structure. By not using punctuation I hope to direct readers to carefully attend to each word — to appreciate the graininess of words.

Reading my poems silently, say, on a bus, a train, or an airplane, and reading them aloud, may be different experiences. The way I've written there's not always a pause intended at the end of the line. Hint: *My poems are to be recited not as lines, but as phrases, and a phrase often overflows the break at the end of a line. I pause and take a breath where it seems natural for me to pause. Another person may pause differently than I do.*

Each single poem is a piece of a mosaic, and it is my hope that the collection of poems form an accurate portrait of consciousness.

My daughter, Jocelyn MacDonald, is a wonderful artist. Her art work graces this book.

— *Tekkan*

Everyday Mind XI

Even though it's
chilly today the
buds are appearing
and I've emptied the
gas from the snow blower.

I am sure the days will be warmer and
There will be tulips lilacs and roses
Within a few weeks but I cannot know
For sure how my business will go or whom

I will meet for the first time tomorrow —
And I can't foresee the quality of
Health of my family and friends — and I
Don't often see what's coming face to face

And am more likely to be surprised and
Unprepared by events — as if events
Came from behind me — and I don't know if
My thinking in the afternoon will be

Optimistic or wearied but I know
I can't escape the tenor of my thoughts.

The future is
unpredictable —
I want to face it
without encumbrance
of mind.

I get distracted when Johnnie won't stop
Yowling for his cat food and he really
Won't stop until I feed him and Kitcat
And Henry too — and they eat before me —

And then I'm thinking about answering
Letters and taking pains to be polite
In my wording while at the same time I
Am trying to remember to get stamps

When arriving at the Post Office but
When departing my hand is reaching for
My keys in my pocket and they aren't there
And I panic because I put them down

Without noticing where I left them and
Now I'm harried and can't find my car keys.

I plan the afternoon
during lunch hour
while feeding cats
eating lunch and
listening to the radio.

From the perspectives of the wizards of
Science who are unlocking mysteries
That were inconceivable a hundred
Years ago the earth is a little blue

Dot whirling in an orbit within a
Larger orbit and expanding from where
The big bang happened some billions of years
Ago — scientists know in billions of

Years the sun will expand to burn the earth
And then to consume the earth within its
Expansion — but these facts have little to
Do with how I may choose to live my life —

The buds are asserting the renewal
Of spring and for me spring is marvelous.

Science informs me
of how exceptional
and fragile the earth is
but doesn't explain the
miracle of life.

The wizards of science are on the cusp
Of the genetic modification
Of the type of food we eat and of the
Quality of human we can birth and

In the future it's possible that we
Will winnow out diseases in the womb
And select for strength and intelligence and
Who could argue against the relief of

The suffering that comes with disease and
Wouldn't it be wonderful to upgrade
Human capability if only
We could identify the genome that

Prioritizes compassion over
Conquest and wisdom over foolishness.

Exponential change
is pitting advancing
technology
against
comprehension.

I transmit thoughts into trained impulses
And my fingers tip tap on tiny keys
And electricity transforms my thoughts
Into bits of information that are

Sequestered into files — and from my phone
I may send my thinking through the air and
Instantaneously it may arrive
On the opposite side of the earth — but

The transmission of ideas — quicker
Than the Greek God Mercury — says nothing
About the foolishness or wisdom of
My ideas — only that thoughts may be

Atomized and launched at the speed of light
As if they were photons of consciousness.

Maybe the cosmos
is full of quanta of
consciousness we
haven't yet learned
to understand.

I bought a mower a year ago and
It was idle throughout the winter but
Today it needed oil and gas and I
Became disoriented because it

Looks different from the old mower — which
I used for ten years — and when I replaced
The air filter I was pleased because a
Screw driver wasn't necessary and

The filter was easy to insert and
I tilted it over to empty the
Oil and the oil didn't empty but
I put in the oil anyway and then

I realized I put the oil where the
Gas should go and now I have a problem.

I pulled the cord
and pulled the cord
but it wouldn't start
and what do I do
now?

I like to parcel my stupidity
Into manageable increments as
It's never a good thing to deposit
An enormous clump of idiocy

Into a single event everyone
Can see — I'd like to be the only one
To recognize that I've done something dumb
So that I may with anonymity

Correct myself before anyone knows
I'm not the genius I purport to be —
And anyway the mower has two holes
And I guess I am not the only one

To pour the oil where the gas should go
And I hope never to do that again.

It's good I have
mechanically
minded friends who
know how to drain
a carburetor.

May is not May without warming days and
The temperature stayed stubbornly cold
Through all of April and we were not free
From the threat of snow so much later in

Spring and the grass is greening and the buds
Are appearing and the birds have returned
From their southern migration and I saw
A robin bobbing on a twig of my

Apple tree and I marveled that the plump
Little robin would choose such a tiny
Twig and the morning is chilly damp and
Overcast and the people I talk to

Are grumbling May is not May without
Warmer temperatures but here we are.

The weather is
an envelope
influencing
my moods.

The coniferous pines and the apple
Trees on my property have become more
Annoying year after year as they scratch
The skin of my arms and shoulders and draw

Blood and as they knock me on the head in
Passing as I mow my grass once a week —
So I've determined to take up a saw
And dismember their lower limbs and bag

The limbs to be disposed of — as I have
Been lazy and have stooped and dodged between
Their branches because I was unwilling
To do a day of extra labor to

Clear my way — but the trees are aggressive
And have taken up available space.

Grasping space and
imposing on each other
is what we do
struggling to
live.

Buds on the trees are unfolding into
Leaves again — for another season of
Breezes — the grass is greening and rising
Up — the sunlight is warming my face for

The first time — the clouds are very high and
Are flowing into feathery wisps in
The currents of the air — and there are tulips
Blooming into splashes of yellow and

Red on the east side of my house — but I
Find myself remembering how high the
Snow accumulated at the end of
The driveway — and I'm anticipating

The mosquitoes and the humidity
And the weekly chore of mowing the grass.

I am a teeter-totter
of sensations
and moods.

A boy on a walk in Iowa was
Curious about an odd-looking stone
And the stone fit snuggly in the palm of
His hand and the stone had been chipped and flaked

And it was weighty and edged and fashioned
For cutting and scraping and maybe the
Stone had laid on the ground for a thousand
Or ten thousand years — was buried under

The dirt and unearthed or was exposed to
Unnumbered starry nights obdurate to
The wind the snow the rain and the glare of
The sun until a boy in Iowa

Noticed an odd stone on the ground — and its
Weight and shape within his palm were perfect.

Stress
hunger
vigor
purpose
intelligence.

My hands are healing from the pokes and scrapes
They got when I was grabbing and sawing
Bending and breaking the lower limbs of
A pine tree that needed trimming — and an

Index finger swelled and itched yesterday
But today it's OK — and the red and
Puffy little wounds that dotted my hands
Have hard scabs today and the soreness and

The weakness in my fingers are gone — and
The larger branches are stacked on the street
And the branches with hard little needles
Are organized in bags along the street —

And this morning my fingers are tapping
On keys and words are forming into lines.

I determine
what to do and
my fingers are
essential
instruments.

My home isn't impressive and wouldn't
Generate much money on the market —
And after twenty years there are many
Repairs I need to do when there's time — though

Some of the problems involve carpentry
And electrical skills that I don't have
And there are handymen but they do need
Paying and I don't have the money so

I am learning to live with a door that
Doesn't close properly — but these are the
Rooms where my children had their birthdays where
They returned after school and I can't know

The details of their secret thoughts but here
Are the rooms that sheltered my family.

The presence
preceding
the absence
sanctifies
a home.

Am I hypnotized believing there is
A separation between my thinking
And behavior and what happens to me
In the events of my life — as if I were

A bystander blindsided by chaos
A victim of random circumstances
Not taking responsibility for
The creative power of my thinking —

Ignorant of how much the world reflects
My attitude — so much so that if the
Patterns of my thinking were different
Experience would be transformative —

Life is wild and unpredictable and
Somehow I am in the middle of it.

My dreams are wild
and unpredictable —
am I creating dreams
or are my dreams
creating me?

While my lilac bushes aren't very thick
It's hard to mow the grass underneath them
Or to rake the leaves surrounding them as
Their branches fork at odd angles and each

Branch will sprout many shoots — and because the
Bushes aren't very thick at a glance it
Seems that nothing is in the way — but when
I approach them suddenly I am stopped

Tangled and scratched and held at a distance —
And if I can reach the leaves under the
Bushes the rake is caught in a stubborn
And interlocking net of sinewy

Defiance as I encounter the wild
And resourceful life of lilac bushes.

I imposed order
and symmetry
on the periphery
with a ladder a saw
and a hedge clipper.

Most of us at the table were members
Of the divorced people's club and we were
Discussing the rites of passage with a
Frightened initiate and opinions

Were offered that it's better not to use
Lawyers because only the lawyers gain
From the escalation of expenses
But sometimes it's true a belligerent

Will resort to lawyers with the purpose
Of exhausting the resources of the
Opponent but it was humbly proposed
Demonization of the other is

Best avoided — negotiation is
Better for the sake of children involved.

A youthful marriage
is a gamble that
compatibility
will persevere
over self-interest.

A radiance is descending from an
Open sky and the grass is rising up
And the buds are unfolding and there is
A single brilliant cloud floating along

And a breeze is stirring the branches — the
Nascent leaves are wafting — and the birds are
Darting about — on the calendar there
Shouldn't be a day designated as

The day that spring arrives because that day
Is unpredictable and today is
Saturday and I'm not strategizing
About making money and I can feel

My body is responding to the sun
With irrepressible liberation

My skin is responding
to warm sunlight
to breeze on my face
and the weight of winter
is evaporating.

Learning how to make decisions that are
Productive and are not self-destructive
Resembles being disoriented
Within my own personal labyrinth

And there needs to be tension in my life
And fear is an effective stimulant
But paralyzing anxiety or
Haphazard reaction is frustrating —

I am grateful for the solitude that
Surrounds me because it's good to listen
To my chattering mind and to burn the
Chaff with the fire of my attention — and

There is a deeper part of me founded
On a quiet discerning watchfulness.

There is a
wellspring of
essential
enthusiasm
directing me.

I don't begrudge the critical voice its
Imposing place within my awareness
Because I need a check on selfishness
And a sense of justice and decency

But it's easy to belittle myself
And to disparage the things I have done
And nothing is more destructive of my
Peace than persistently negative thought

And the daily tenor of my thinking
Has the capacity to destroy my
Chances for happiness if I give my
Punishing monologue too much power

But I don't have to be alone in my
Thinking — I can always talk with my friends

Without
circumspection
gentleness
patience
love I'm
lost.

Time is segmented artificially
Into seconds minutes hours and into
Days weeks months and years — but from another
View segmenting a day is natural

For we are bound to a sense of time marked
By the rising and setting sun and by
The repetition of seasons with the
Flowering trees and the melancholy

Of the turning of the autumn leaves — and
We are captivated by the knowledge
Of death beyond which there is only a
Terrifying ignorance as each of

Us knows every human face is destined
To dissolve and disappear into dust.

I accept ignorance
and choose to believe
life resurrects
consciousness continues
and there is no ending.

Metamorphosis is a fancy word
Meaning the morphing of one form into
Another and it happens all the time
And the sun is the instigator and

The sky is its theater — and the clouds
May gather and darken quickly and a
Sudden downpour of rain may transform the
Day — and every year there are the few days

When the sun showers warm sunlight again —
No matter how long the dreary winter
May persist — and the leaves appear — and the
Flowering trees bloom again with white pink

And red blossoms — and the tulips had a
Blooming and now their petals have fallen.

I morph from
expectation
confusion
frustration
curiosity
elation.

A friend was on a dig in Israel
With his friend Ofer at an ancient fort
And Ofer unearthed a hammered golden
Ring that came from the height of the Roman

Empire two thousand years ago and
Ofer wore the ring on his pinky for
Eight years until Ofer was asked about
The ring at a conference and to my

Friend's amazement Ofer gave the ring to
The person who asked about it because
Ofer said the ring was taking too much
Of his consciousness — as an example

Ofer enjoyed an unexpected gift
And he learned how to pass the gift along.

The gift is an
unexpected
liberation.

The apple blossoms were in the puddles
On the pavement after the pelting of
The rain — looking like the confetti on
The street after a parade — but we missed

The parade this year as the blooms were just
Starting to appear when an overnight
Downpour broke the connections of petals
With the trees and I feel a little sad

That the joyous parade of my driving
By the flowering trees has passed me by
This year because I love seeing the blooms
As a celebration of beauty that

Always accompanies the return of
Spring and the resurrection of the trees.

But now I see
many of the trees
have yet to reach
their full flowering and
I'm just being gloomy.

It's been chilly far later into spring
Than at any time I can remember
And for the last few days it's been raining
But the leaves are almost fully grown and

They appear gradually but when they
Are grown they are always freshly pristine —
And on any day there are details that
Need attending to with people and work

And it would be easy to overlook
The return of the leaves for another year
Of productive sunlight — but what I love
Is the peaceful sound of the breeze stirring

In the branches and sighing through the leaves
Which suggests there's no need to be anxious.

The breeze in the leaves
is background music
whispering and
peaceful.

A student doesn't have to travel far
To find the lessons that are genuine
And the suggestion I read this morning
Was that there are only two emotions —

Fear and love — and that irritation and
Jealousy and anger — or gratitude
And forgiveness and curiosity —
Derive from the one root or the other

And it's easy to live ignorantly
To be arrogant and to believe I
Am doing as I should be doing and that
Anyone in my place would do the same —

And there is no end to indulged anger
But there is resonance in gratitude.

The resonance of
gratitude
forgiveness
curiosity leads
to a better life.

It's easy to think my thoughts are private
And that I can't be blamed for angry thoughts
But anger isn't easily contained
And my thinking ripples into the world

And the world ripples in response to me —
And so I watch the quality of my
Thinking and I know when my balance is
Off — and it is possible to become

Quiet through the practice of watching thoughts
And I can fortify my consciousness
With persistence and patience — because I
Know that I will feel differently in

A little while as circumstances change —
And I see the world never stops changing.

There is so much
going on all around me
in a single moment
I can't possibly
comprehend.

The wind in the leaves is too rough to be
Poetical and the sky is filled with
Such gloomy and low-hanging clouds moving
Quickly and raining spontaneously

And the air has been stubbornly chilly
Too long into spring for my preference
But the leaves are fully grown and the birds
Are darting about in a violent

Wind — like so many other things in life I
Don't get to choose what the weather will
Be and I have to make do with what comes with
A daily view of metamorphosis —

Is it silly to wonder whether the
World would exist without my being here?

I guess the question
depends on whether
my consciousness is a
drop of a bigger
consciousness.

I am a drop of consciousness and what
I don't know extends beyond what I do
And I may easily be discouraged
When I am feeling lonely and afraid

And when I am isolated sometimes
I create explanations in my head
About why a person said hurtful words
That impacted and summoned my anger

Or when I can't find a way into a
Conversation among my friends I may
Believe myself unworthy of friendship
And I am lost in silent arguments

So it is my practice to forget that
I am only a drop of consciousness.

A drop of
consciousness
needs to find
a way to flow
in the river.

I won't say that Johnnie is becoming
Seven pounds of nuisance because saying
So isn't nice — but just between the two
Of us — he is — as I was enjoying

A dream this morning immersed in a world
Of swords and spears and warriors when I
Heard the intrusion of a yowling cat
Demanding food outside of my door and

He's becoming more insistent over
Time and he's starting earlier in the
Morning and I can exclaim JOHNNIE NO
But Johnnie won't stop until he's been fed

So I get up and carry him to the
Bathroom deposit him and shut the door.

Johnnie
should think
about his
behavior and
whether it's
propitious.

To me the blooming of cherry blossoms and
Lilacs are worthy of celebration
And I don't do anything overt to
Mark their appearance except to notice

How they lighten my spirit — and the breeze
Will envelope their sweet scents and waft it
Away — and very soon the breeze will take
The delicate petals and flowers and

Scatter them on the ground — and I wonder
How do the flowers blossom when through the
Winter the branches are bare and the trees are
Frozen — and I marvel at the absence

Or the emptiness from which everything
Appears and to which everything returns.

When blossoms
appear the bees
get busy — but do
they also rejoice?

There is a shifting in spring into a
Sunny brilliance when the light sparkles on
The river as the dreary weather has
Dissipated — and the sun becomes a

Magical source of resurrection — and
The dandelions and the creeping Charlie
Appear in my yard — and the trees by my
Driveway present their apple blossoms — and

I'm not sure whether the newly grown leaves
Are brightest in the spring or whether their
Dramatic reappearance lends them a
Magnificence that wears off over time

But the sighing of the breeze in the leaves
Is whispering such soothing assurance.

The curving of space
by the gravity of the
sun tips the earth
around the sun
predictably.

A storyteller assumes the powers
Of a deity weaving with threads of
Meaning into the stories of a Queen
Of a dragon and of a bastard who

Is really of royal birth — but once the
Tale's been told the mystery is
Gone and the fate of the actors is known
And the retelling can only rehearse

A familiar conclusion — but we need
Storytellers and if we are smart we
Will choose the tellers who inspire and
Ennoble because our authentic lives

May be dispiriting and it's good to
Weave with the threads of hopeful energy.

Dissipating or
accumulating
enthusiasm is
determinate.

Writers used to be confronted by the
Emptiness of a sheet of paper but
Today the paper has been replaced with
A blank computer screen with a blinking

Cursor — but the challenge is exactly
The same — what thoughts do I have this morning
That are worthy of communication —
Invisible raindrops are falling from

A gray sky and my circumstances are
A little gloomy but I'm not bound by
Moodiness because writing poems is
An enthusiasm generating

Machine for me as I've discovered a
Method for grasping satisfaction.

There are roots of
curiosity and
gratitude about
simply living that
flower.

I'm in my element most of the time
And swimming along without a worry
As I wake up early every morning
And after doing some chores I will sit on

A cushion and meditate for a while
Which gives me an indefinable sort
Of energy that mitigates the wear
That comes with the ordinary ups and

Downs — and I love the freedom that arrives
With the sunlight of morning clarity
When my mind percolates with probing thoughts
And I may indulge curiosity

Until I see another damn letter
From the Internal Revenue Service.

Suddenly I'm
a goldfish in
a little bowl with
an idiotic cat
after me.

When I close my eyes when facing the sun
I see a marvelous red light that is
The sunlight filtered by my eyelids — and
My face is bathed in the beating of the

Sun and after a few minutes I am
A little dizzy — and the red sunlight
Warming my face helps me to imagine
Myself a tomato under the sky

With nothing to do all day but listen
To the drone of cars and machinery
In the distance and absorb the force of
The persisting sunlight enveloping

And tranquilizing me in unceasing
Dissolving forgetful meditation.

Raindrops
inescapably
pattering
my face
would be
difficult.

Politics is an insider's game and
The players rely on the fact that most
Citizens don't have the inclination
Or the knowledge to follow the details

Of issues and it's advantageous to
Accuse opponents of dishonesty
And to smear their reputations with the
Most outrageous slanders — and the players

Know that they are lying — and perhaps they
Smirk at notions of Hell — but once they start
There can be no relenting from lying
Accusing and empty posturing because

The momentum is unforgiving and
They are terrified of exposure.

They are riding the
tiger of politics
desperately
afraid and
grasping.

Not every thought I have is worthy of
My attention and some thoughts are burning
Cinders that light upon my skin and hurt
And I have to practice flicking those thoughts

Away instantly or otherwise I
Will find myself swirling inside of a
Malignant obsession with vacant eyes —
And I can't at the moment prevent a

Perception from rising within my mind
But with the focus of my attention
I can practice letting go of anger —
And what I choose to say or do is a

Confirmation of my intentions and
Being careful is the art of living.

The harmony of
living is a happy
mixture of what
happens and how
I think about it.

The art of living is the releasing
Of dispiriting thoughts and the seeking
Of inspiration and when I saw the drops
Of water hanging from the crooks of my

My apple tree after a rainy day
In February I was astonished
By the sight of the hundreds of drops of
Water refracting the sunlight in a

Tree in a season when usually
Everything is frozen and burdened by
The snow — I realized that the world is
Fluid and unpredictable — even

In midst of difficulty there is
The surprising poignancy of beauty.

Anticipating
inspiration is
like snatching
a bird
in flight.

The freedom of mind to see a blue jay
A red wing blackbird or a cardinal
And to see them without a thought getting
In the way is wonderful — I touch them

With my sight on the fly and I am left
To wonder at the beauty on the move
About me — I like to leave my thinking
Behind me for a while because it's so

Easy to be obsessive and then
I am not using my eyes properly —
And when I am not the center of my
Attention the unfiltered impact of

The world makes its influence felt in waves
Of difficulty sorrow and beauty.

My friend Judy
directed me
to a silky
little bird — the
cedar waxwing.

The blooming of the lilacs has nothing
To do with me as I am not lifting
A finger to make it happen as the
Purple flowering appears briefly once

A year and the sweet scent doesn't travel
Far and when I am properly focused
On the details of my business and the
Common unpredictability of

Cooperating with people lilacs
Are of no assistance to me except
That I look forward to their blossoming
And their scent in the middle of winter

And their coming and going brings such joy
And joy in passing is worth indulging.

Lilacs of
various shades
are predicable
in a fluid and
disappointing world.

While walking from the height of the north hill
Down through Stillwater and south along the
River I ascended up and across the
Magnificent Crossing Bridge spanning the

River — and a thought came to mind that I
Could read one day's collection of essays
From America's major newspapers
With the intention that I would quote the

Snarky and accusatory writing —
I would write an essay exposing
The corrupting and dispiriting weight
Of commentary that Americans

Are reading on any random day — but
I realized that's the nature of news.

Americans artfully
spanned a river valley
at a great height and
Americans have an
appetite for venom.

A dragonfly has extraordinary
Eyes that wrap around its head and allow
It to see behind and below on the
Fly and each eye deploys thirty thousand

Lenses and each lens captures an image
Of the fluid world and they combine to
Give it extraordinary sight — and the
Dragonfly can follow the flight of a

Fly and with four angled wings capable
Of hovering and flying backwards it
Can snatch the fly from the air and slice it
With its mandibles and eat the fly while

Hovering — and it sees the colors of
Ultraviolet light that I can't see.

But I can't
imagine getting
many dates if
I had a dragonfly's
head.

I had the curiosity and time
And a search on Google informed me that
The ruby-throated hummingbird flies straight
And fast — but can stop instantly — hover —

And adjust up and down — hummingbird hearts
Are beating twelve hundred times a minute —
And they are breathing two hundred fifty
Times a minute — and they are licking their

Nectar ten to fifteen times a second —
And I can hardly believe the essay
Saying that a dominant hummingbird
Has the gumption to chase the jays and crows

And the hawks away from a feeder once
The hummingbird has taken possession.

I could put up
a hummingbird
feeder and
hummingbirds
would come.

The bee hummingbird is an exquisite
Native of Cuba with fluttering wings
Iridescent feathers and a pointy
Little beak and the bird and its nectar

Are coincident because one could not
Exist without the other — just as I
Could not exist without the sky the rain
And the earth — this is what the earth has come

To with hummingbirds and flowers and rain
And people — as we are emerging out
Of the trillions and trillions of degrees
That was coincident with the little

Space that was expanding rapidly that
The scientists are naming the big bang.

The bee hummingbird
and I are a
continuation a
permutation of
the big bang.

See what the cosmos is capable of
On the earth as I am an awakened
Drop of consciousness under a sun — and
As a drop of consciousness absorbed in

Kaleidoscopic rivers and oceans
And drops of rain I am at home in the
Liquidity of the earth as the earth
Is incarnating and dissolving forms —

And I can appreciate the flouncing
And the prancing of an opalescent
Peacock and the slithering sinuous
Motion of a garter snake — and in the

Brilliance of an open summer sky I
Spot the floating of a cottonwood puff.

I wonder whether
consciousness comes
within waves of
appearing vanishing
quanta.

It was time to feed the cats before dawn
And Kitcat wasn't in the house and the
Only explanation was he got out
When the door opened without being seen

And he disappeared once before last year
On a day that became rainy and I
Worried about him because he was never
Outside by himself and I wasn't sure

He'd be OK — now for the second time
He escaped and stayed away for the whole
Day — and like before in the early hours
Before dawn he yowled at a window and

I opened the door and in he came and
He flopped on the carpet triumphantly.

Maybe he pressed
open the latch
of the screed door
by standing on
hind legs.

The beating of my heart and the burning
Of the sun are cooperating — a
Supernova seeded the cosmos
With the elements of life eons ago —

And gravity formed the planets and tipped
The planets into orbit around our
Sun — and gravity crushed the mass of
The sun igniting nuclear fusion —

And a sun burning and a heart beating
Are spontaneous and simpatico
Are a mixture of the vast and minute
Collapsing into curiosity —

My body is an outgrowth of cosmic
Proportions — but where do questions come from?

Am I beating
my heart or is
the cosmos
beating it?

There are assumptions within my thinking
That are unnoticed within rhythms and
Rhythms of thinking — and sometimes I am
Able to recognize that my thinking

Is convincing me that everything is
Chaotic and that I need to impose
Myself and make things happen and thereby
Gain satisfaction — and sometimes I can

Recognize that what is emanating
In the form of my rhythmic thinking is
Resonating into what's happening
Around me — and that sometimes there is a

Painful dissonance and sometimes there is
Harmony — while everything is flowing.

Thoughts are like raindrops
blowing on a lake —
with few harmonies
with many chaos.

Are the burning sun and a beating heart
Separate phenomena or are
They continuous with each other
Proceeding from the original source

That is called the big bang — though however
It happened there couldn't have been a sound
Because for a sound to register there
Needs to be an atmosphere to transmit

Vibrations and there needs to be ears and
Minds to transform the vibrations into
What could become a bang — and however
It happened there was nothing beforehand

But afterwards something was expanding
Radiating vibrating emerging?

Sun burning
heart beating
ears hearing
mind thinking —
are they all vibrations?

My head is a gourd of the cosmos — and
Thoughts are emerging from behind my eyes —
Or at least that's how it appears to me —
And scientists have discovered that the

Vibrations in my brain are transforming
Photons arriving from the sun into
My perceptions of colored light — and if
My brain were not transforming vibrations

There wouldn't be any light at all but
Only transitory vibrations through
Emptiness — and it's hard imagine
There being neither brightness nor darkness

And it's hard imagine the absence
Of colors — but that's what emptiness is.

My cosmic gourd is
creating
sight
sound
smell
touch
taste
questions.

While driving around and observing the
Familiar scenery on the highway
And in Stillwater I am listening
To Alan Watts on a disk saying that

I am casting a net over the world
Dividing and classifying the world
Measuring and quantifying the world
While everything is continuous — and

In the natural world there is no such
Thing as an inch — or a mile — or a line
Of longitude — and time doesn't come in
Seconds or minutes but — truly — the trees

And the horizon wiggle — the birds wiggle
And people are especially wiggly.

Can I pick up
an inch by the
edge from the
ground and
pocket it?

The trees were quiet a moment ago
But now they are sighing in a breeze —
Streaming gray clouds were converging and
Concealing and the sun — then they were

Dispersing and revealing the sun — and the
Light was momentarily brilliant — but now
The gloom and the chill are returning as
The clouds are obscuring the sun again —

My hands were on a steering wheel as I
Was turning corners on the streets driving
To arrive at my desk — I was typing and
Deleting words uncertain about my

Direction — but now I've discovered a
Pattern while hunched in a chair composing.

Quiet and sighing
shadow and light
restless confusion
settling thought
satisfaction.

I'm not enlightened but would like to be
And I know — because I'm listening to
Alan Watts — that craving enlightenment
Becomes a guaranteed impediment —

And Alan is insisting there's nothing
I can do and no where I can go to
Penetrate the mystery — and Alan
Is saying that it may take thirty years

Or three seconds — while the evidence is
Everywhere before me — and having a
Good laugh afterwards is a natural
Result — and Alan is suggesting that

Secretly I don't want to wake up but
When I really really do — then I will.

Alan has a way
of simplifying
and clarifying
and I can't stop
listening.

A teacher in Japan talked about the
Unborn mind that is given by parents
To their children that is always present
And the unborn mind can be distinguished

Said the teacher when the students are in
The dharma hall and are listening to
A teacher and a sparrow twitters and a
A crow caws and the birds are heard as a

Crow and sparrow without difficulty
And no effort was made to hear them and yet
They were heard and this is the eternal
Mind that doesn't struggle to exist and

In America after four hundred
Years I am puzzling over his words.

Zen Master Bankei
pointed out
unhindered
bare awareness.

What does the air do to a butterfly
As it emerges from a chrysalis
Not having been a butterfly before
And discovering that it has wings — and

Does it fall and flutter as it falls or
Does it arouse itself and beat the air
With its wings to rise into the air for
Its initial flight — and is it a strain

On a butterfly's heart to push down on
The air as its beating heart is in sync
With its sashaying manner — and is the
Air the same air the gliding eagle or

The acrobatic swallow knows or is
It living in a different cosmos?

What does the
butterfly think as
it encounters drops
of rain and a
boisterous wind?

I've lived most of my life without knowing
When during the day I am most awake —
And maybe meditation is helping —
And maybe playing with words is helping —

Because I have to be flexible to
Play with words — but now I am using the
Tides of my mind — seeing clarity come —
Feeling energy — anticipating

The insights — like snatching a bird in flight —
But then I endure the ebbing of my
Energy and the ensuing dullness —
There is pleasure in surfing the tide and

In cultivating inspiration but
Then I have to let energy go.

When I am
naked in the shower
warm cascading water
summons enthusiasm
and clarity.

"Good friend for Jesus sake forbeare,
To dig the dust enclosed here.
Blessed be the man that spares these stones,
And cursed be he that moves my bones."
—William Shakespeare

When I was a student in England I
Went on a solitary pilgrimage
To the Church of the Holy Trinity
In Stratford-upon-Avon to visit

The earthly remains of the poet whose
Plays and sonnets had so inspired me
And I didn't really know exactly
What about his writing had taken root

But the inscription on his grave was a
Clue sparking recognition today — I
Adore his piercing concision and his
Passion and the play of images and

Personality — that all he gave me
Were the words — and his imagination.

When I imagine
Kings and Queens —
and clowns — it's
Shakespeare I
rely on.

I have lived with the peonies on my
Property for twenty years as they are
Rooted with the daylilies within a
Circle of largish rocks I labored hard

To establish — and my ex-wife planted the
Peonies — and I didn't know the name
Of their kind of flowering though I did
Admire their pink lush beauty — but there

Were many years when I overlooked their
Blooming and this spring I was surprised at
Their presence and noticed the oddity
Of peonies — that their overlarge blooms

Bend their blossoming to the earth giving
Them the appearance of bashful women.

Embarrassed
beauty is an
alluring ploy
mesmerizing
lustful bees.

The names we give to things are a gloss of
Our humanity so that when we see
The planets and the moons of our solar
System we say — in the manner of the

Ancient Greeks and their deities — there is
Saturn and there — Saturn's largest moon — is
Titan — and we could not do otherwise
Because the things we see must be given

Their names and thereby comprehended — and
Our sight has extended into space and
We can see that the lakes of Titan are
Liquid methane and we can understand

That the cosmos is inhospitable
To life — outside of the earth's atmosphere.

The big bang
was silent because
without an atmosphere
and without ears
there is no sound.

There is the precarious time of night
After midnight and much before the dawn
When — if I find myself awake — there is
Great difficulty in falling back to

Sleep — because once I start thinking about
My difficulties the debates I have
With me do tend to become obsessive —
But last night I heard the minutest whine

Of a mosquito coming nearby and
Going away — and once I heard it by
My ear and I slapped — and smacked my ear —
And it whined about my ear again and

I slapped and smacked my ear again — and then
I laid awake vigilant and vengeful.

Don't tell me to —
take it easy — because
that's a fatuous
phrase designed
for idiots.

I take a considerable amount
Of bother to arrive at my office
With an air of serenity about
Me by meditating beforehand and

I arrange my schedule to allow
A sacred hour of quiet so that
I can apply myself to poetry
And I settle within a comfy chair

And gaze longingly out of my widow —
And with fingers poised over my keyboard
And with my thoughts beginning to pop the
Damn phone tears my attention away and

All I hear is a recorded message
Saying — stop and listen and don't hang up.

Robocalls
everyday
like mosquitoes
are snatching
my composure.

I'm thinking I am at the center of
The cosmos and maybe everyone is
Also thinking they are at the center
Of the cosmos — which prompts the question where

Can we find the circumference — and maybe
There isn't a circumference — and I am
Questioning whether the fire knows it is
Burning itself and does the water know

It's quenching itself — and do I really
Know how I am beating my heart and how
I am inhaling and exhaling air
With my lungs — or is there a broader part

Of everyone that does these things without
Having to know the things we are doing?

And maybe
consciousness doesn't
need to remember
much beyond the
present moment?

There is a flux of consciousness in a
Day with the impetus of clarity
In the morning and the dissipation
Of energy and optimism in

The afternoon and there are the rhythms
Of a beating heart and circulating
Blood and breathing lungs continuing with
No conscious direction and there is the

Drowsy transition into sleep and the
Eerie unpredictability of
Dreams — and where would I go if I went to
Sleep and didn't wake up and what would it

Be like to awake after not having
Gone to sleep — which is what everyone does?

Fluxing
rhythmic
automatic
cosmos working
me.

The rose bush was bordering the concrete
Patio in front of the door to my
House when we came twenty years ago and
It has needed the trimming I didn't

Do until the previous year — because I
Am easily distracted and sometimes
I am lazy — but I did expend a
Little energy pruning the dead wood

Away — and now I see the rooting of
The bush has moved from its early spot to
Sprout between the cracks of the concrete and
It is a gnarly and persistent plant

Worthy of its thorns and maybe I would
Not have noticed but for its blossoming.

The rhythm at
my home is
apple
lilac
peony
pink roses.

Light and sound envelope me in waves and
The thing to know about the waves is that
There is the crest and the trough and if
I think about things from a view of an

Ocean of particles I'm swimming in
Sometimes I am an aggregation of
Particles and sometimes I dissolve into
A waving ocean vanishing and then

Appearing again — and I tend to think
Of moments as the building blocks of time
Marching to a conclusion but then I
Can see the cycles of the orbits and

The seasons as more compatible with
A crazy wavy unceasing cosmos.

Van Gogh observed
wavy reality
before quanta
became a knowable
thing.

My ability to think and move is
Not the same as a leaf emerging from
A bud and unfolding — is not like a
Peony bloom appearing in June — and

I tend to believe that trees and plants and
The sky and the river are part of the
World — and that I am something apart that
Was summoned into the world to play a

Part like an actor on a stage — and my
Soul comes from and returns to another
Realm — but maybe the world is growing me
And I am emerging out of it — like

A thoughtful peony blossom and a
Conscious cosmos is seeing with my eyes.

Maybe the cosmos
grows consciousness
like it grows
gravity and galaxies.

I like to write about the cosmos and
Peonies but it happens when I am
Waiting for the words to fit perfectly
Into a pattern of sound and grammar

And syllables — that come together like
The pieces of a puzzle — suddenly
My attention is ripped away by the
Ringing of the infernal phone — and from

Experience I know I'll likely hear
The tinny voice of a robot with a
Message of no interest to me — and I
Am primed to growl — hello — and if there's

A silence or a click when listening
To the receiver I will just hang up.

This is a cosmos
mixing peonies
and robocalls —
mosquitoes and
roses.

I sit facing my window with the sun
Rising with a wide brim straw hat grateful
That I am here with a clear mind shielding
My eyes from the bountiful summer light

And relishing the tipping point between
Coolness and the warmth of the asserting
Sun and I don't have to know very much
About what anyone else is doing

At the moment and don't have to wonder
What I'll be doing in a couple of
Weeks as I'm beginning to believe my
Beating heart and seeing eyes and warming

Skin and the birds the dragonflies and the
Sun are a perfect sphere of consciousness.

Sun penetrating
heart inaudible
ears absorbing
the printer humming
the aquarium bubbling.

If I look at the world with fresh eyes could
I forget about the differences
Between the outside and the inside of
Me — could I dispense with my habit of

Fixing on the proximity between
Me and others and could I stop taking
Possession of what's mine as opposed to
What's yours — because I have a lifetime of

Practice of making distinctions and of
Constructing an identity with the
Urgency of ignorance and fear — and
I suspect everyone else is playing

By the same rules with a ferocity
That makes playing the game so dangerous?

Just for a moment
could I dissolve
proximity and names and
even words and with a
finger touch the moon?

There is a humongous hill of ants near
The cottonwood where I was watering
The grass and I didn't think much about
Them except to see that their colony

Is extending around the cottonwood —
And then I was attending a meeting
Of my friends and waiting for my turn to
Speak while wearing a silk Guayabera

Shirt when there was a tickling under
My shirt and across my belly and I
Felt the tiny feet and knew that an ant
Was ascending to my collar bone as

I was attempting to listen to my
Friends — and not to wiggle scratch and grimace.

I am not usually
aware of the
fine hair on my
belly — but the
ant reminded me.

With the abundance of the summer sun
I can mow the grass following supper
When the leaves are sparkling with the sun
And there is not a time when I am free

From doing the chores that come with living
And the imperative of getting things
Done is something I do without thinking —
And the prominence of the summer sun

Is a pattern of a lifetime that is
Akin to a heart beating and the lungs
Breathing — as it is a pattern within
Patterns I am not manipulating —

But I'm taking the time to absorb the
Warm embrace of the reliable glow.

I imagine
myself a
marshmallow
browning outside in
and inside out.

I've been trying to keep up with my chores
And mowing the grass and feeding the cats
And watering where the grass seed was laid —
And by rushing from chore to chore I did

Prodigious work in a couple of days —
Just so I could have a carefree Sunday —
But there was rain and wind in the morning
And my cottonwood did what cottonwoods

Do — break apart and drop branches — and now
I have a tangle of weighty thick limbs
To dispose of — and how will I do this

Unexpected task without giving up
Something else I would rather be doing?

I suspect the
cottonwood is
my guru today
playing a game by
dropping hints.

My eyes are seeing perfectly well what
Is in front of them — there is rain and wind
And the trees are tossing about — but I
Can't see what's behind my eyes and can't see

The back of my head — and it would be a
Hoot to be a perfect sphere of vision
So that I could see the top of my feet
The ceiling the carpet and the doorway

Behind me — but even then there would be
An empty spot inside my spherical
Eye — and usually I don't notice
What I would call my hole of consciousness —

There isn't light or darkness inside my
Head where my thinking is percolating.

The emptiness
where my thoughts
come from is the
emptiness where the
cosmos comes from.

The emptiness behind my eyes is not
Something that I can think about because
I cannot see or grab hold of it — and
It is not even a thing — it is a

No thing — I can see the tip of my nose
And I can turn in any direction
And enjoy a field of vision that is
Limited — and with technology I

Can view galaxies and with books I can
Play with ideas that are based on things
That are within the galaxies — and I
Generate my emotions dependent

On my relations with people or things —
But I know nothing about emptiness.

Except
everything
comes from
emptiness.

There was a day forty years ago when
I was a grunt on an asphalt driveway
Crew preparing the ground for the layer
Of underlying rock that we would lay

And the natural mixture of rocky
Soil needed to be broken up so that
A foundation could be made — and they gave
Me a pickax with permission to wreak

Havoc — in an ecstasy of labor
I discovered how to swing the ax with
The continuous movement of my feet
And with the furious melody of

Unceasing circling destroying blows
Which was a workingman's enlightenment.

I became the
embodiment of
righteous
disintegrating
force.

There was a reason for the pickax that
Day as the tractor couldn't get at the
Spot and the work had to be accomplished
By shoveling and the ground was as hard

As cement and the flat end of the ax
That angles outwards is designed to drive
Into the earth and explode the earth with
The removing swing of the ax — and the

Ground was broken to bits — and shovels could
Be thrust in to remove the rocky dirt —
And on that day my body was youthful
And a joyous fierceness awoke in me

That I didn't know I was capable
Of — and decades later I remember.

I swung the ax and
Willie the crew chief
on the tractor
called me
 John Henry.

Would it go to my head if I stood at
The top of a mountain wearing a wing
Suit surging with adrenaline seeing
The immensity of distance before

Me and taking a of leap of terror and
Joy to fall gracefully among rocky
Precipices as if I became an
Eagle plunging in and out of alpine

Shadows prepared for a sudden death in
Exchange for a rushing simulation
Of divinity — would I glory in
The experience and be compelled to

Do it again — to be soaring again
Exploding the bounds of humanity.

Flying in a
wing suit
would be a
high I'd never
escape.

I was minding my business eating lunch
And listening to the radio when
A grape escaped my grasp and rolled away
And I straightened my back and gasped because

This sort of thing has happened before with
Peanuts and grapes — and I know as far as
Potential trauma goes a lost grape is
Small potatoes — and a missing grape is

More of an inconvenience as I
Just don't want to step on a grape with a
Bare foot — so I scanned the carpet and the
Wood floor without success — and turned about

In frustration putting my life on hold
Searching searching for the purple nuisance.

I slipped into
denial saying
there is
no
purple
grape.

I don't have to worry about why the
Cosmos has peopled the earth with humans
Because I am here as one among the
Billions of us — and I don't have to think

About my eyes and ears and tongue to make
Them work as they see and hear and taste with
No effort on my part — there is sight and
Sound and taste and consciousness coming with

Life — and even with my dreaming at night
I cannot separate myself from the
Nature of my being — I breath and the
Sun burns and I can imagine the crest

Of sunlight perpetually breaking
Over the earth — turning the night to day.

I don't have to
worry so much
because I'm coming
to believe consciousness
is indestructible.

Johnnie the cat in his elder years has
Developed a habit of yowling for
His food as he anticipates being
Forgotten and it is damn annoying

To hear him — and he won't stop when I say
NO — and it's better to ignore the noise
While feeding him but yesterday I sang
Daba daba daba daba — eeyoow —

Daba daba daba daba — eeyoow —
Daba daba daba daba — eeeyooow —
Daba daba daba daba daba
Eeeyooow eeeyooow — so together we had

A little harmony and a test of
Dominance and Johnnie was the winner.

I'm cranky
but he thinks
he's starving.

How does my head look to my eyes — and may
I turn my head to see it better — or
Is it always beyond my seeing — or
Perhaps when I'm seeing pink rose petals

Dry on the concrete and the daylilies
Beginning to bloom — and see my mother
Becoming frailer with age in the home
Holding so many of our memories

And possessions — perhaps I am seeing
What there is to see — that everything lives
To blossom and pass away — and perhaps
It's better to relax and flow with the

Current — as I am a story I tell
Myself on the way to another birth?

But perhaps my
head contains the
cosmos that keeps
creating visions?

There are different rhythms to life and some
Are profound and seemingly eternal
Like the tide coming in and going out
In response to the movements of the moon

And the passing of a person into
The elements is a seemingly cruel
Transition because we don't remember
What the experience of dying is

Like — but the fear of the unknown can be
A source of stimulation because I
Learn this is a world where everything is
Changing into something else and maybe

I can find encouragement in the thought
Death is only a season of living.

The sight and song
of an indigo bunting
on the fly is a
glimpse of ephemeral
beauty.

Without the sensation of touching the
Sun would be neither warm nor cool and
Without the propensity of seeing
The sun would be neither bright nor dark as

I create the waves of light with my eyes
And I manifest the warmth of the sun
With my skin — and I appreciate the
Music of Beethoven with my ears — and

A peach would not be peachy without my
Tasting it — because it is my body
That makes seeing hearing touching tasting
Smelling and comprehending possible —

I am not even lifting a finger
And yet I'm bringing the cosmos to life.

I don't have to
worry about birth
as it keeps on
happening.

Henry is a white cat with orange spots
And he is missing the tips of his ears
Because they were frozen off while he was
Living outside in the winter — and a

Friend allowed him inside and took care of
Him — and I have had him for many years
And he developed kidney disease so
Every morning with my hand I scoop him

Up from bed and take him to the kitchen
Where from behind him I leverage his face back
And squirt some medicine down his throat with
A syringe — which he doesn't like so much —

But the sticky stuff keeps him from getting
Constipated and permits him to eat.

He makes
growly
raspy
curmudgeonly
commentary.

I have been driving around and seeing
The scenery of city streets and of
The highway and listening to disks of
Alan Watts who was a beatnik guru

Telling me that within my head there is
Hidden a hintergedanken — meaning
That there is something that I know but will
Not admit — and it's not a trivial

Thing like knowing I need to lose weight or
To pay for the registration of my
Car again — and it's not admitting that
I'm a drunk because I've already done

That — this hintergedanken is so much
More fundamentally liberating.

Alan is exposing
the riddling tricks
of gurus so maybe
he's playing a
trick on me.

There is the nagging intuition that
Life is more than the satisfactions of
Eating and having sex but I can't put
My finger on what's the bigger deal and

Alan says that I am continuous
And interdependent with everything
Else — so much so that if you were not you
I would not be who I am — and Alan

Is saying that part of me knows the whole
Cosmos is seeing with my eyes but when
I am trying by an act of will to grasp
Enlightenment frustration arises —

The hintergedanken is Alan's way
Of suggesting wisdom before knowledge.

Driving around and
listening to Alan
inspires
unexplainable
joy.

When we drunks talk among ourselves with the
Intention of perpetuating our
Sobriety sometimes one of us will
Confidently repeat a point — as if

By the elaboration and by the
Assertion of his words he could transform —
And from my experience I know that
I need to listen carefully to the

Words that come out of me — and it is true
Sometimes I can talk myself into a
Better way of feeling as my words give
Me the leverage I need to strengthen

My intentions to remember that a
World of misery comes with the first drink.

Some of us
are treading
water over a bottomless
pit and the words we
choose are pivotal.

An onion is a handy symbol for
Life because there are the layers of skin
That can be peeled away until at the
Center nothing remains — so the thing to

Do is to cut the skins and mix them with
Other ingredients and savor their
Taste and digest the onion — there is the
Illusion that I can peel away the

Surfaces of things to find a hidden
Truth after which there is satisfaction —
Can I savor the skin after skin
And be satisfied with the taste of life

Without grasping for explanations — as
If my tasting weren't miracle enough?

With telescopes and
microscopes we chase
the cosmos and it
keeps on
evading.

There was a time my Dad told me that he
Didn't believe in an afterlife and
That when we die we go to a void — and
His saying so was a revelation

To me — that he was a Christian who was
Ministering to a congregation
From a pulpit while not believing in
The resurrection — that he viewed himself

As a Roman stoic who thought that the
Consolations of the gospels were a
Crutch for a weaker sort of people — and
I understand the vehemence of his

Need to be important and the stress he
Placed upon having righteous opinions.

Today I believe
he frightened
himself to
death.

There is so much sunlight in July from
The early hours of the morning on
Into the shadowing of the evening
That the grass and the trees and the sky are

Transformed into a glowing presence and
Today there is an occasional breeze
In the leaves and the air is suffused with
A dry heat that is a pleasure to feel

And everything that I see is tinged in
A yellow light and the air is alive
With flying insects from the smallest gnats
To the speeding flies vanishing and three

Crows are flying in circles and chasing
Each other twice among the quiet leaves.

After forty minutes
of meditation all
my sensations are
drinking in a
summer morning.

I don't know what a Roman stoic
Was and I don't believe my Dad really
Did either because he could only have
Read about them in books after they died

Thousands of years ago and the earth has
Moved on and so my Dad was expressing
A rejection of his perception of
His intellectual surroundings — which

Is sad — because an unresolved fear of
Oblivion drove his thinking — like a
Person who is slowly drowning — while I'm
Trying to awake and discover that

The void is pregnant with consciousness and
Birth is a gift that keeps on happening.

My dad was terrified of
graves but with practice I don't
need explanations and
rationalizations as
persisting joy arises.

I return to the question does the world
Exist apart from me or do we both
Arise together inseparable —
While the patterns of my living with my

Perceptions and reactions and all the
Elements of my identity are
Destined to dissolve as transitory
As a season's leafing — along with a

Listing of accomplishments that only
I am capable of remembering with
Dubious accuracy — all the while
There is an irrepressible birthing

Going on coming from a void bestowing
Such rejuvenating forgetfulness?

Am I really by
myself beating my
heart or is the
whole cosmos
beating my heart?

The sun is baking my head while I am
At my desk and it's taking an effort
Of will to focus my thoughts while it is
So much easier to notice the heat

About my face and neck and under my
Arms as I am beginning to sweat in
The moisture of this morning's heat — while the
The plants outside the window are growing

Riotously after a night of rain
And thunder with the radiation and
Radiation bearing down on the land
And fetching the biting mosquitoes and

Flies and irritation is easy and
So I'm just going to be irritated.

At my desk I raise
my feet and lower
my toes — my clogs
fall off and my feet are
bare joyously.

Six months ago the temperature was
Twenty below zero but today I
Am wearing clogs — which are a glorious
Invention — because they allow all the

Benefits of going barefoot without
Drawbacks — as I enjoy lifting my heels
While sitting down and feeling the heat of
The summer air envelope my ankles

And by lowering my toes the clogs will
Drop and my feet obtain liberation —
I don't have to poke my skin by walking
Over rocks — and don't have to smear my feet

With dirt — and if a pebble gets under
A foot I tilt and the pebble falls out.

The clogs that were
left behind at a hotel
and given to me are
two sizes too big — so
I am duckish.

When I am thinking about myself and
All the unfortunate things that happened
To me and about how a certain girl
Treated me it is natural to fall

Into a gruesome mood as if I were
A whirlpool swirling uselessly and
Wasting the marvelous unfolding of
The cosmos as it appears at the moment

So it's much better to see the cobwebs
In the corner of a window wafting
In a breeze that the air conditioner
Is raising or to enjoy the design

Of my clogs that I may wear or dispense
With — indulging my fickle summer moods.

There is so much
possession and
defending going
on in thinking
about myself.

I put my chin in the cup of my palm
While looking out of the window — and I
Am thinking of nothing especially
Important — and the sun is declining

Behind me as the green of the leaves and
The white of the clouds and the blue of the
Sky are untouched by the evening shadows —
There are the hums in the room emitted

By the refrigerator the printer
And the aquarium — particles are
Cresting from the sky and bouncing off of
The clouds and leaves and I am creating

A spectrum of light — and vibrations are
Undulating and I am making sound.

Rippling thoughts are
leaving traces
in the form of
some words on
paper.

The gray of the clouds is pregnant with rain
And the rain may burst at any moment
And I'm waiting for something to happen
Anticipating a sudden downpour

And the tiny white blooms of the clover
Are ascending above the blades of grass
And there is just enough breeze stirring the
Leaves to make the quiet more prominent —

There's not a bird in sight — not a squirrel
Anywhere — a hundred thousand blades of
Grass — a hundred thousand leaves — are waiting —
Gloom is descending — chill is engulfing —

Butterflies and dragonflies are grounded
And not a drop of rain has fallen yet.

Dark patches of the
overcast sky are
moving swiftly.

Bayport Minnesota and Hutchison
Kansas are alive in me — not as they
Are today but how they were forty and
Fifty years ago — and I remember

My first friend Eric — though probably I
Wouldn't recognize him today — and there
Are many painful memories as it's
Easy to recall my disappointments —

And as I keep going on and on there
Is more and more to remember though I
Suspect I've forgotten most of my life —
And I wonder whether I am choosing

What to recall and what to forget or
Is memory something that just happens?

I am happy to be
a soap bubble person
ready to disappear
to be born again
for another game.

There are islands of shade under the pines
The apple trees and the cottonwood but
The remainder of the lawn is exposed
To the blaze of the sun as the gripping

Treads of the front two self-propelled wheels of
My mower are pulling me along and
Covering the grass with two whirling blades
As I am enveloped and baking in

The moist air of a July afternoon
Happy that I had sawed off the lower
Limbs of the apple trees and the pines so
That I could move rapidly without a

Hindrance and to impose my will and to
Establish order on my property.

Kentucky blue grass
creeping Charlie
dandelions
and clover are
all the same to me.

The blazing sun
is concealed by
threatening clouds
as heat continues
into evening.

— *Tekkan*

Everyday Mind XII

The sun this morning
is fierce enough
to burn its shining disk
right through a layer
of clouds.

I am wearing a straw hat with a wide
Brim shielding my eyes from the rising sun —
And if I had a boss he would not be
Happy with me because I look to be

Almost completely idle — my fingers
Are poised over the keyboard but I'm not
Typing — or I am flicking my fingers
Out in sequence from a fist as I am

Counting syllables — sitting at my desk
Facing a window — attempting to catch
Something extraordinary in the air
Or a usable fact from Google but

The sun is rising in an open sky
And what's so interesting about that?

The sun's not rising —
the earth is rolling in
the direction of
the sun at about a
thousand miles an hour.

This morning was darker than normal and
I noticed the clouds were heavy and low
As I went about brushing and feeding
My cats and cleaning the cat litter box

And my mind became fully awake as
The warm water cascaded over my
Naked body in the shower — and I
Explored possibilities for the day —

I heard the rain begin to fall through the
Open windows of my room — as I was
Sitting cross-legged on a cushion in
The dark — the rain accumulated in

A pattering of drops falling on the
Roof and grass — rising to a crescendo.

Yesterday afternoon
a moist heat
clung to my skin but
this morning there is
enveloping coolness.

When the sun is up on a summer day
And the shadows of the trees and buildings —
And the shadows of the people walking
Are making such a sharp contrast — and when

The leaves are rustling in a wind and
The river is undulating and the
Steel frame of the Lift Bridge in downtown
Stillwater is brilliantly reflecting

The sun with razor clarity — then the
Shadows offer no relief from the heat
Of daylight and then who notices the
Silhouettes of the shadows shrinking to

A minimum under the midday height
Of the summer sun burning so brightly?

The blazing sun
would be beyond
experience
unknowable
without
shadows.

I was helping Jocelyn and Eric
Move to Minneapolis by backing
My car up a hill of a driveway to
Their apartment — when I came to a

Point of turning to avoid another
Car — and I had to guess direction
Because I can't see over the rear of
My car — and crunch — I hit the other car —

I jumped out to inspect the damage which
Was nothing to the other bumper and
I really did think there was no damage
To my bumper either — and as no one

Was watching I rubbed out the scuffmarks and
Decided to pretend nothing happened.

Jocelyn saw a
dent and Eric laid
on the ground and popped
the fiberglass corner out
and I professed ignorance.

The car that I tried to avoid belonged
To my ex-wife Yoshiko who was there
To help move our daughter Jocelyn — and
I know how much Yoshiko cherishes

Her car — and there was the time in Japan
When I ate a glob of wasabi — which
Is a very hot sauce meant to be used
With sparing discretion — that I thought was

Guacamole — with the result that I
Nearly blew my head off — and the mishap
Is never forgotten — and the story
Is often retold — so I could assume

That my accident while backing up would
Live on in infamy forevermore.

While backing up and
having to guess at
distances I knew
the difficulty
but I was cocky.

[Yoshiko is pronounced Yosheeko]

Just by virtue of taking a risk I
Propelled myself on an unexpected
Rollercoaster ride of daring and of
Panic and of the fear of exposure

And of sudden relief when I believed
I escaped and nothing had happened — and
When I wet the tips of my fingers with
Spit and rubbed out the scuff marks truly my

Calm was reestablished — but Jocelyn
Saw right away what had eluded me —
That there was a fresh dent in the bumper
Of my Toyota Corolla — I was

Even a little jealous that Eric
Knew how to pop away the evidence.

Nothing more was said
and now I will see
if Jocelyn is really
reading the poems
I've been emailing.

It was about 3 in the morning I
Think when I got up from bed to go to
The bathroom to pee — which is my habit —
And then I returned to the bedroom and

Closed the door — and then either I can fall
Asleep again — or if unlucky — I
Can't and I toss about for the rest
Of the night — but this night I noticed a

Rustle at the open window and realized
Kitcat was in the room — but I was too
Tired to rise again and grab him so I
Just tried to sleep — and I almost managed to

Doze off but I was held in suspension
Because I knew Kitcat was in the room.

Kitcat is a
rascal and a fool
and he is most attentive
to outside noises
and most jumpy at night.

I think there was a sunlit beach with a
Plethora of bodacious women in
The skimpiest of bikinis in the
Dream that I left behind me when I rose

To pee — and now I was on the edge of
Rejoining them with hardly a whisper of
A breeze in the room when at the open
Window just above my head I heard a

Shifting of the curtains and I knew that
Kitcat was alert and surveying the
Night for danger — in the middle of a
Careless jumble I almost managed to

Conk but part of me was aware that a
Tense and nervy Kitcat was in the room.

Was I dreaming
of restless leopards
on the savanna
of Africa or was I
elsewhere?

There is a window on the south side of
The room and a window on the east just
Above the head of my bed and in my
Dazed and dozing state I knew that Kit was

Slinking between the windows as the air
Was cool and tranquilizing — which always
Makes me think of those midsummer night dreams
That Shakespeare goes on about — and I was

Drifting and swinging as if I were in
A hammock and then I felt that Kitcat
Was standing on my legs and he broke the
Spell of slumbering and I awoke and

Knew that the opportunity was gone
And the only thing to do was to write.

I recognize when
the facility for
putting words together
arrives — and I won't
squander opportunity.

There is a window on the south side of
The room and a window on the east just
Above the head of my bed and in my
Dazed and dozing state I knew that Kit was

Slinking between the windows as the air
Was cool and tranquilizing — which always
Makes me think of those midsummer night dreams
That Shakespeare goes on about — and I was

Drifting and swinging as if I were in
A hammock and then I felt that Kitcat
Was standing on my legs and he broke the
Spell of slumbering and I awoke and

Knew that the opportunity was gone
And the only thing to do was to write.

I recognize when
the facility for
putting words together
arrives — and I won't
squander opportunity.

I first heard about meditation by
Reading Hermann Hesse's Siddhartha
In my high school library — and I was
Captivated by the mysterious

Spiritual journey Siddhartha embarked
Upon — that he left a luxurious
Life in a quest for enlightenment in
The jungle of India two thousand

Years ago — that he bore the hardships of
Living naked in the rain the heat and
The cold and that he endured the rigors
Of hunger — that he would willingly do

This by straightening his back and crossing
His legs — and by going into a trance.

I wanted the
superhuman
experience of
enlightenment
and the trance.

Hermann Hesse planted a seed that flowered
When I arrived in Japan twenty years
Later to be an English teacher and
A friend introduced me to a temple

And I was initiated into
The way of Zen — and I learned how to sit
Quietly with a straight back and crossed legs
While the monks and the visitors sat for

Many hours of a day for seven days
Of meditation — and the Zen master
Said that I had entered Buddha way
And that the point of the practicing is

To awaken and I could not fail if
I were wholehearted in my efforts.

During seven days
of enveloping quiet
there were bells
and drums and people
stepped carefully.

I discovered that my idea of
Meditation as a trance I enter
Or a spell I cast upon myself was
Mistaken — and that the purpose of the

Posture and the surrounding quiet was
For me to experience clearly the
Ordinary operation of my
Mind — so that I could see the restlessness

And could understand the fabrications
That I invent to explain the world to
Me — so that I could appreciate that
So much of my thinking is leading me

Astray — and that I am the author of
My dissatisfaction and confusion.

The world becomes
a funhouse mirror
of the way I am
thinking and
feeling.

My mind is a bowl responding in the
Dark absorbing vibrations and raising
A radiant sun — and creating the
Jubilant celebration of the birds —

Straightening my spine and crossing my legs
I don't have to do anything extra
Because my retina and synapses
Are inventing the sunlight — my eardrums

And synapses are devising bird song —
Because without the bowl of my mind the
Vibrations in the air would obtain no
Response — and without the vibrations in

The air my magical bowl would become
Empty — and what would emptiness be like?

My mind is a bowl
inventing the cosmos —
the cosmos is
vibration
creating
me.

I was sitting at a booth selling books
And watching people going by and most
Were indifferent but some would stop and
Talk for a while when a girl walked by who

I was happy to give two years of predawn
Attention to — when we talked for an hour
On the phone every day — while I was in
Bed — and we shared our emotions and talked

About the people we knew and I learned
How intoxicating conversation
Could be — enough to occupy me for
The rest of my days — but she kept walking

And I didn't try to stop her and I
Am not even sure whether she saw me.

She reminded me
I can choose to
reinterpret
events endlessly
but I'd rather not.

When I put my thermos of coffee down
And can't remember where I put it or
When I suddenly meet someone I know
And I find I can't remember his name

My thoughts are condemning of myself for
My poor memory — but then there are the
Regretful experiences when I
Invested so much hopeful emotion

With perhaps some unwise expectation
And a good measure of blind fantasy
In a pursuit that I knew was risky — then
I find that forgetting isn't easy

And the weight of unresolved memory
Is a ferment of continuing pangs.

Dropping rain
bubbling springs
fleeting rivers
falling water
boundless oceans
clouds drifting
have no memory.

These are the riddles of consciousness to
Wonder — was there a beginning — is there
An end — did I originate at birth —
Do I have a destination — because

Everything is moving — the galaxies
The stars and the planets are orbiting —
Starlight penetrates the cosmos in waves —
Subatomic particles are spinning —

The sun enfolds my face in a warm glow
And sometimes I feel perfectly at home —
But sometimes I am overcome with a
Sense of urgency that I have to make

Something happen — but then I realize —
I'm not at all sure what I really want.

Today I'm
drinking coffee
reading essays
absorbing news
answering mail.

How weary would I be trailing behind
Me the unerring memories of lives
With the intervals of prosperity
And the endurance of the heartbreaking

Turns of fortune — when there were too many
Disappointments — when in my misery
I could not stop comparing myself with
Others who were luckier — and what would

Remembering a lover who is lost
To me forever be like — as I could
Not forget her gentleness and voice —
Wouldn't I be better off forgetting

Every detail of my experience
Whether I was jubilant or burdened?

Maybe misplacing
my car keys
is a touch
of grace?

Where is he? I asked as I hadn't seen
Him for several weeks and I missed his smile
And his warm intelligence — and she took
Me aside where the others couldn't hear

And answered that he's been on a bender
And she doesn't know what to do and would
I call him she asked as she knows he and
I are friends — I remember he isn't

The first alcoholic she's been involved
With and I recognize desperation
When I see it — set apart where others
Can't see it — because with the others she

Is smiling and putting on a brave face
As I see both of them are suffering.

"Yes I'll call and
remember you
didn't cause it
can't control it
can't cure it."

There is freedom in the moment to think
About whatever comes to mind and not
To dwell upon what's beyond my sight and what's
Surpassing my ability to change

As I could be preoccupied with an
Alcoholic friend who can't stop drinking
Or I could be wondering how my son
Is faring in Alaska but after

Reaching out and not hearing news there is
Nothing more to do — and every moment
I could be encumbered uselessly or
I could deploy my daily routines and

Drink my coffee and edit some essays
And lose myself in intriguing details.

A gray sparrow
is hopping in the
hedge outside the
window a couple
feet away.

When I doubt myself the people and the
Events of a day become funhouse mirrors
Reflecting back to me my supposed
Image distorted by what I think should

Be happening — and a debate ensues
Wherein part of me justifies myself
While the other part wants a convincing
Satisfaction that's unobtainable —

But I've experienced enough to know
The internal dialogue is useless
And a friendly honest conversation
About any topic that comes to mind

Dissolves the mirrors and clarifies my
Vision — and life returns to normalcy.

A distorted
perspective dissolves
with friendly
conversation with
another person.

Down corridors and into the rooms of
What are more often than not churches — and
This was true even for the nine years that
I lived in Japan — I will go to meet my

Fellow alcoholics who are trying
To stay sober — and for more than thirty
Years we have shared the camaraderie
Of getting to know each others' stories

And of learning the tricks of avoiding
The first drink — which is the drink leading to
Catastrophe — and you wouldn't know it
Being with us as a nonalcoholic

And witnessing our banter and laughter
That some of us are fighting to survive.

At some point we are
desperadoes and despite
our laughter we need
to remember the
initial desperation.

As we were walking Jane took off her shoes
And went barefoot on the sidewalk — which I
Could never have predicated and I said
So — and then she deliberately sped up

With her long legs flowing forcing me to
Keep up — and I inquired wasn't she
Worried about stepping on debris on
The concrete — and she scoffed saying there was

No debris because someone always comes
By to sweep it away especially
Near the state capitol building to which
I replied there is debris too small to

Be seen everywhere except on mountain
Tops and even there the rock will crumble.

She said something
unremarkable
but she did
get the last
word.

I want the child in me to emerge as
Often as possible as I let go
Of the tensions and the expectations
Coming with experience as I give

Myself the quiet allowing my thoughts
To settle down — seeing so to speak the
Operation of my thinking — that all
The emotions come and go if they are

Given the room to express themselves and
Seeing so to speak I don't have to cling
To a point of view — and when I let go
I can dwell again in child-like wonder

As life becomes a ceaseless adventure
Full of unpredictable potential.

So much tension is
expectation run
amok dreading
unavoidable
conclusions.

The serried fields of corn are fully grown
The days are almost equally balanced
Between showers of the rain and sunshine
And in the afternoon there is the moist

Embrace of summer humidity and
The air is filled in the evening with
The pestering of flying insects but
Here and there about the country in the

Upper reaches of the trees there are the
First appearances of the red leaves of
Autumn and there is no denying now
That darkness is encroaching day after

Day further into the daylight and yet
Winter seems an impossibility.

Something about the
constancy of the clouds
sailing across the sky
merges the seasons
together in memory.

I dreamed of being a mite on a walk
Across the palm of a sleeping human's
Hand encountering successive creases
And deep lines in the dark — and I could choose

To follow along the pathway of one
Of the smaller creases while indulging
A belief that a destination were
Ahead — but then eventually I

Would come across the deepest of lines and
Be forced to descend the depth with an
Ominous premonition that I was
Being channeled having only the choice

Of moving forward to uncertainty
Or of stopping and awaiting my fate.

But perspective
easily shifts with
the brilliance of
the morning light.

Sometimes when entering a room I will
Discover that I've forgotten why I
Came — and at other times I will see a
Familiar person and realize

That I can't remember his name — and then
I think myself unworthy and wonder
Whether I should stand within the tall grass
To attract the ticks — but sometimes I will

See or hear something triggering a
Memory and precipitously I
Am reliving the circumstances
And rehashing the arguments of a

Cherished grudge of a dozen years ago
And I think forgetting would be blissful.

Forgetting and
remembering
are things I do
without thinking
much about them.

The sun of this morning brightens all of
My sensations and fosters clarity
And all the ups and downs involved in a
Typical season dissolve at sunrise

As the sun is a worthy symbol of
My sphere of consciousness bringing to light
Everything it touches enlivening
And enthusing with the combustion of

My attention — and problems left over
From yesterday are child's play to resolve
When energy and clarity are merged —
But I also need to recognize when

My energy is ebbing because then
The shadows assume their rightful places.

Shadow surrounds
incandescence —
forgetfulness
accompanies
clarity.

There's a short sleeve shirt that's a pleasure to
Wear once the mornings become chilly in
August because it's a thick weave and has
The substance to keep the warmth inside and

It is a black silk shirt embroidered with
Navy blue tracery and luminous
Silver dragons that for some reason leads
Me to think of stardust and gravity

As if it were a representation
Of the primordial cosmos swirling
And coalescing into galaxies
Containing the code of consciousness and

When wearing it I feel like royalty
Representing the life of the cosmos.

It was an eight-dollar
purchase at the
second-hand store
called Good Will in
Stillwater Minnesota.

I want to rethink my attitude towards
Forgetfulness — while stipulating that
Forgetting a name or misplacing my
Car keys will always be irritating —

Because on occasion when I awake
In the night remembering my regrets
Experiencing again frustrations
Searching again for consolation in

The darkness where imagination runs
Wild even as the recreation of
Vanished opportunity is tempting
I know my memory is distorted

And what could have happened differently
Isn't worth the useless speculation.

Forgetting is
opening
sleeping
dreaming
spontaneously.

I remember Zen master Harada
Saying if you know something — forget it —
Which sounds simple but is complicated
Because I don't like the embarrassment

Of forgetting someone's name — but then I
Wonder whether Harada was meaning
To forget the embarrassment that comes
With forgetting names — that I shouldn't be

Clinging to the idea that I am a
Person who habitually forgets
Names — that I should relax and not worry
No matter how many names I forget

Because if a person is important
Certainly I will remember the name.

I guess remembering
and forgetting go along
with the dissolving
and rebirthing of
everything.

Temple Hosshin-ji

Monks in the Zen temple were serious
During continuous meditation
And a strict schedule was enforced with the
Striking of the bells and wooden clappers

And there was no unnecessary talk
As we sat and ate and walked about in
Silence — as we were pursuing the trick
Of liberation desiring to cast

Away our bodies and minds to become
Enlightened penetrating instantly
The boundary between ignorance and
Certitude — study the moment — practice

Wholeheartedly — master Harada said —
Obtain the posture — and forget yourself.

Master Harada struck
the tatami with a staff —
saying with wholehearted
effort you cannot miss.

I frequently visited *Hosshin-ji*
Doing continuous meditation
Because I had a yen for Zen wanting
Liberation thinking I could grasp it

Through determination and focus — and
After six days of sitting I achieved
Such an energetic clarity that
Only comes from strenuous effort with

The knowledge that I could never do more
Through force of will — but my endurance of
The lotus posture wasn't enough to
Evade my ego — which I felt as a

Burden — so with alert exuberance
I left a little disoriented.

The exhortation of
Harada Sekkei Roshi
resembled the hectoring
of my wrestling coach —
had I failed?

I was an English teacher in Japan
And wasn't a monk but could arrange to
Visit four times a year — and I didn't
Wear the formal black robes but instead I

Gallivanted in my black pants and a
Black sweatshirt with a blue scarf unaware
Of the delicate sensibility
Of the monks passing silently about

With stern faces until the tallest monk
Daigaku Rumme came and leaned over
Me tucking the blazing blue of the scarf
Inside my sweat shirt and thus harmony

Was restored in the temple as I learned
That blue is distracting in the Zendo.

It's surprising
how often words
are unnecessary.

There is a curious rumbling of
Thunder in the distance while the sky was
Resplendent an hour ago — and now the
Prospect of an open morning is gone

And the gray of the clouds is an almost
Certain indication of rain coming —
Which would not have been a surprise if I
Were watching the satellite images

But sometimes I like the weather to come
Upon me unannounced by news people
Because surprising weather consists of
Raw experience — as a mixture of

Beauty alternating with the burdens
And unpredictability of life.

I don't dislike the rain
as the sound of rain is
pleasing — and soothing
spattering and drumming — and
I don't have to shovel rain.

When rummaging in the garage I found
Two sets of wind chimes I had put aside
Because they both were missing the part that
Catches the slightest of winds moving the

Center disk striking the chimes and making
The air resonate — and I shook the chimes
And heard the familiar falsetto
And the bass again after their many

Years of silence — their hooks under the eaves
Were there and I hung the chimes along my
Roof again resolving as I did to
Refashion the wind catchers when I could —

Windy days and chimes remind me of how
Simple and pleasurable beauty is.

A home
and
chimes
are
musical.

Master Harada reminded me of
My high school wrestling coach inspiring
Extraordinary efforts through the force
Of his personality — and he spoke

With admiration of a Zen master
Of a century ago who marshaled
The monks and pronounced that whomever had
Not grasped enlightenment by the end of

The practice period would be buried
Alive — and master Harada didn't
Reveal how many were actually
Covered up so I presume after the

Appointed time the temple was filled with
Realized followers of the Buddha.

Earnest effort
and humor
inspire
good practice.

Harada was reputed to be a
Teacher of koans — embedding nagging
Riddles within a mind — by remarking
With wholehearted effort attainment is

Like hitting the ground with a staff and you
Cannot miss — and those who fail deserve to
Be buried alive — and with the correct
Posture of mind in an instant you may

Forget yourself — and he energized and
Directed me and I struggled silently
By maintaining a straight back and crossed legs
Hour after hour day after day month

After month — laboring and desiring
To extinguish desire by force of will.

My wrestling coach
never imposed
enticing and
impossible
situations.

Mowing the grass weekly was what I did
Because I had to and viewed it as a
Chore but now I'm liking the exercise
And am circling the flower gardens

I established by placing large rocks in
Ovals about the yard — mowing around
The rocks once and twice and thrice pretending
I am a star spiraling about the

Milky Way rotating further out with
Each pass participating in the swirl
Of gravity grateful to have a small
Portion of the earth to care about and

Not presumptuous that the living earth is
Something that is permanently possessed.

I pass over the
entirety — about the
gardens apple trees
cottonwood pines and the house —
with a pair of whirling blades.

Saying hippopotamus is lovely
And saying hippopotami is a
Wonderful variation with the
Added benefit that people may not

Understand the meaning — and I enjoy
Pronouncing hippopotamus with an
Ascending inflection as if I were
Asking a question — and it's fun to say

Hippopotamus while putting on a
Stern expression because it makes such a
Curious contrast with the gaiety of
The word — and you should try saying every

Syllable pausing in-between because
You'll find it difficult not to speed up.

It's regrettable
there aren't many
occasions in
America to say
hip-po-potamus.

In the last few day of summer I took
A walk to the horizon and on the way
There were the grasshoppers and crickets and
When I reached the mile long avenue in

The sky of the Crossing Bridge with the broad
River a hundred feet below me I
Wondered how the construction workers spanned
The empty air with steel and concrete when

There was as yet nowhere to stand — and on
Returning I thought of the sayings of
The Zen masters — that I do not exist —
That my hand is illusory grasping

At smoke — that I can't discover the way
Either by doing or by not doing.

A thousand years ago
the Chinese monks walked great
distances searching for a
master of Zen who could
spark them.

I am a sphere of consciousness shining
The light of my awareness over the
Events of every day — and even when
Remembering I am remembering

Presently so what I remember is
An illusion — and when indulging my
Memories I am recreating what
Happened and using memories often

To make myself happy or remorseful —
And in continuing if not careful
I will be beholding a series of
Funhouse mirrors each as distorted as

Another as the emotion of the
Present moment is most dominating.

The sky and
the diversity of
clouds are more
worthy of
attention.

The monkey bars in the empty park were
Inviting — could I grip and hold and
Swing my body's weight with alternating
Hands propelling myself to the end — yes

I could and did — in junior high school our
Gym teacher led the boys onto the bus
While we were wearing our white t-shirts
Shorts and — for the first time ever — jockstraps —

While going to the Old Athletic Field
And preparing for competition
Gangly and short and chubby and nervous
And unprepared for public exposure —

The adrenalin of excitement and
Embarrassment was intoxicating.

I can do the monkey bars
today but my fellows
outdo me by taking
expensive vacations in
Paris or the Bahamas.

There are ten thousand leaves moving in a
Gentle breeze in the September light of
A morning sunrise as the peaking of
The summer heat is passing by and the

Season is approaching a natural
Harvesting of the growth of the rooted
Plants — and the light shining on the green leaves
Is a sight worthy of noticing and

Cherishing — as the leaves are bearing the
Bite marks of the insects and soon the leaves
Will be turning into autumn colors
And yet the quality of September

Light is most beautiful I think as the
Light isn't starkly bright but is glowing.

Shadow is lengthening
further into daylight
and shadow is gathering
underneath the trees when the
sky is overcome with clouds.

When the cosmos was spontaneously
Birthing there was no bang because there were
No ears to hear the sound and no air to
Transmit the vibrations — and even now

Outside of the earth's atmosphere within
The vacuum of space the original
Silence is predominating — but I
Am a drop of consciousness and the

Earth also is a drop of consciousness —
And when I am sitting quietly and
Attending to my thoughts and listening
To the sounds of the birds or of the rain I

Am not separate from the primal
Impetus but continuous with it.

From the silence
reverberations of
pattering rain and
singing birds have
emerged.

The nastiness of the political
Discourse broadcast on the cable channels
On the radio and in newspapers
Is frightening — and because I attend

To the details of events and issues
I can identify the smears the lies
The distortions and the propaganda
I can see how the youngest voters are

Programmed to hate before they understand
The history and the complexity
Of government — as politicos are
Masterful at deceiving innocence

At manipulating ignorance and
At camouflaging insincerity.

Once a person is
poisoned with aggressive
talking points reasoned
dialogue becomes
almost impossible.

I practice Zen to separate my
Emotions from the vitriol of
The cultural and political war
That is raging across America

As I am writing and publishing on
Current events — and having already
Informed myself about the destructive
And dominating aspects of money

Power and government nothing about
Today's poisonous discourse surprises
Me — except perhaps the extent to which
Politicos are eager to involve

Children from the grade schools through the high schools —
Teaching partisan ideology.

No segment of
society is free of
the taint of politics —
not even the *dharma*
in Zen centers.

No matter how justified it appears
With every ounce of vigor to oppose
The haters in society using
Accusatory language is risky

Because hating will mirror hating in
Opposition with the escalating
Rhetoric transforming into vengeance —
And there are battles to be fought and won —

But once belligerence has taken root
Distinguishing honest disagreement
From malicious intent is difficult
And vengeful words are poisonous to those

Who say them because we don't realize
Hating haters turns us into haters.

Governing involves
the use of power and
the allocation of
precious commodities
conjuring disagreement.

It is a goofy frog painted yellow
And green that is hanging on the outside
Of the door that's an entrance into my
House — it was put there by my ex-wife whom

I allowed to live with me for six years
Following our divorce — though there really
Wasn't a reconciliation but
Only a toleration that has worn

Out — that has resulted in me asking
Her to leave the home — which grieves me to do —
Which she is unable to understand —
I hope her leaving eventually

Will be seen to be the best outcome for
Both of us — even if it's painful now.

Yoshiko bought
the frog with
the script saying
welcome.

A generation has passed — the children
Are grown and gone — my home is cluttered with
Useless things — and I want to rent a large
Dumping container and like a cyclone

Progress through the bookshelves closets cupboards
Wardrobes chests of drawers — look under the beds
Into boxes untouched for years — enter the
Spare room and drag the mattress up the stairs

Out through the door — I will break the couch
We had such trouble getting into the
Basement into pieces and throw it out
Bit by bit — but perhaps I'm not prepared

To be so determinate when finding
The wedding and the honeymoon photos.

In a corner of
the ceiling there are
bits of crepe paper
streamers left from
a birthday party.

Thousands of memories of Yoshiko
Are embedded and latent in my mind
Ready to emerge and surprise me — as
Someone in a conversation mentioned

The Renaissance Fair and I remembered
The day we went as a family when
She decided my presence in the group
Wasn't wanted and she excluded me —

And I realize the emotion of
What I thought was guilt — in asking her to
Leave — is probably grieving — as I had
Already lost my family many

Years ago — as our togetherness was
A façade concealing my loneliness.

Guilt and grieving
are mixed and
justification
isn't necessary.

By the river in downtown Stillwater
There is a planter full of purple and
Red petunias blooming in the sunlight
Escaping my notice until today

I plucked a blossom — felt the velvety
Texture — inhaled the petunia scent —
Red and purple richness — soft petals — the
Balm of inhaling petunias — surprised

Me — and yes I noticed sunlight playing
On the surface of the river and the
Dewdrops sprinkled on the newly mown grass
But they were insignificant today

I asked a passerby for the flower's
Name — and now I know about petunias.

My tongue
dances when
I say
petunia.

After thirty years of living every
Drawer and closet is full of stuff some of
Which I haven't handled for twenty years —
Like the fifty-year-old sleeping bags I

Inherited from my parents — I am
Preparing to be a cyclone tossing
Everything time has rendered useless but
I am dreading triggering the landmines

Like deciding what to do with the
Sturdy bags we used on our honeymoon
How to dispose of the wedding photos —
It would be better not to look at them —

I will be sorting the debris of life
Touching items — enduring memory.

I am preparing to
rediscover
relive
reflect
renew.

When I am unable to sleep sometimes
At night I will hear the horn of a train
In the distance — and when I am sitting
Before dawn absorbing the sounds through my

Window I will hear traffic moving on
The highway and on the city streets — then
I remember meditating before
Dawn in a temple in a city on

A bay by the Sea of Japan where I
Heard the traffic in the distance on
The highway — people are always moving
Restlessly in the dark in the distance

Adopting a direction — departing
And arriving at their destinations.

People are moving
in the night covering
distances going
somewhere in
solitude.

Waves of light are speeding while waves of sound
Are leisurely and our classic Rolls Royce
Is loitering on the highway passing
Tractor-trailer trucks over the rolling

Hills as we are seeing the fully grown
Rows of corn and grass moving in a breeze
And shining in the mild light of early
September — as we are progressing to

The Log Cabin Family Restaurant in
Baraboo Wisconsin again for our
Periodic business meeting where we
Discuss the shifting fortunes of our work —

A political movement has died and
We are conniving to launch another.

We are caught in a swirl
orbiting and waving
ceasing and beginning
conversing and silent
continuing.

No — the supervisor said — we need the
Security code that your ex-wife made
Twenty years ago before we will stop
The billing and will discontinue

Your Internet services — and thank you
For your patience — but you are sending the
Code to my ex-wife's email address and
I don't have access to that address now

I replied — and I'm waiting for it to
Arrive by mail but it's not coming and
I don't want penalties for late payments
And don't want my credit rating ruined

And why can't you be adaptable and
Send it to my current email address?

Rules are rules and
it's easy to
initiate services
and hard to break the bonds of
connectivity.

On the refrigerator there is a
Piece of paper left behind announcing
The award that my ex-wife Yoshiko was
Given for being the best employee of

The month — and I know she's a hard worker
And that everyone who was working at
The hotel where Yoshiko cleaned rooms has
Left the hotel — even the owners and

Managers — have gone on to better jobs
Years ago — and I don't know where she is
Don't know whether she is struggling or
Doing well — she wouldn't believe me if

I told her but I grieve for the hardness
Of her life — and want her to be happy.

I will enclose the
award in a box
containing photos
of the family growing
until today.

I don't remember what the arguments
Were about but only that they happened
And that they happened for thirty-three years
Within intervals approximating

Companionship and even happiness
On occasion when I was proud to be
A Dad and a provider — but trauma from
Her childhood never healed — her anger and

Her accusatory mentality
Are a burden I can no longer carry —
Who's right or wrong is trivial — the fact
Is we don't get along and we need to

Live separately for our closing years
And maybe we can both be happier.

Living together for
six years after
a twenty-seven marriage
ended in divorce
was a mistake.

There is space within my house created
By the dispersal of my family
And the only disagreement now is
Where the cat litter box belongs and that

Will involve negotiation between
My felines and me — I am adjusting
To the reliable quiet within
The rooms I know so well — I am aware

Of the potential for remorse and grief
To take over the decisions about
What to keep or to let go — the present
Is pregnant with possibility and

I think the sky is a good example —
Cloudy or empty — it is full of light.

Life-giving energy
permeates being
constantly
vibrating
here.

In September I notice the little
Kids on the corner waiting for the bus
To take them to school — remembering as
I do the many years I took the bus to

School — recalling the apprehension and
The unpredictability coming
With leaving home for the first time and of
Encountering the presence of strangers —

And today I notice the little kids
With a father or mother beside them
Undergoing as they are the first pains
Of separation realizing the

Bonds of parentage — that no matter how
Long I live I will always be a Dad.

Attending grade school
junior high and high school
for the second time with
my kids I watched them
grow and leave home.

A zebra was injured and unable
To rise from the grass of the savanna
When in the distance a lion appeared
And the lion began to approach at

A trot — the features of the lion's face
Expressed a stern intensity and the
Mane surrounding his face was flowing with
The motion of his advance — while the tall

Grass obscured the movement of his legs the
Shaggy mane and face were fascinating
Coming from a distance as his face was
Alert and fixed with brutal intention —

There is an awful and mesmerizing
Ruthlessness in an apex predator.

I remember being
fascinated by the
gleaming brass of a
lion's face fashioned
into a door knocker.

I am leaving my windows open just
A little above the sill overnight
Regardless of the chill encroaching in
The night — because I am holding on to

The ease of the warmer days and there is
A visceral revulsion to the coming
Season — in the morning I am walking
About in bare feet — though my ankles are

Cooler and the wood boards of the floor are
Are beginning to impart a bite through
The soles of my feet and up my legs — I'm
Not going to shut my windows and seal my

House until it's really necessary
When I have to resort to the furnace.

The afternoon sun
is warm and so many
green leaves are
reflecting a
golden light.

Love and the absence of love are woven
Together as I thought I knew what was
Missing and told myself for years if she
Weren't here I'd have what I want — but I am

Discovering all the time and beneath
My conscious awareness I was blaming
Her for an absence of love while knowing
She was wounded and suffering from her

Torturous thoughts as I was defensive
And withdrawn and was incapable of
Providing beyond the shelter of a
House which really didn't amount to a

Home — and now hunger is mixed with numbness
And I have no idea what I want.

There is love
to be seen in people's
faces in their movements
and in the generations
of children.

We arise from the waves and orbits of
Particles spinning and winking in and
Out of existence — from the emptiness
From which everything emerges — and we

Arise on a rotating and orbiting
Planet in a solar system within
A galaxy along with the other
Galaxies as all the galaxies are

Expanding — moving and thinking within
The cycles of seconds and minutes and
Hours days seasons and years — and it's easy
Not to notice the segmentation of

Time and distance are artificial tools
Measuring underlying emptiness.

The movement
of second and hour hands
around a clock are
only meaningful
to human minds.

The outermost layer is thin and dry
And is not edible so I make a
Cut and peel the layer off — I cut the
Whole in halves with a heavy blade — and with

My fingers holding the ends together
I cut across a half to make slices —
Then comes the tricky part as I'm holding
The slices of the half together with

My fingers as I'm cutting lengthwise
And aiming to produce smaller sections
And to put them in the crock pot when it
Just happens that my fingers fumble and

Everything falls apart forcing me to
Say — I can't cut an onion gracefully.

The second half is
especially
troublesome
as my eyes are
burning with tears.

There are three curio cabinets in
My home holding porcelain figurines
Of Chinese monks and stone frogs untouched for
Twenty years because the keys were broken

Or lost — the dust has settled within them
Coating the glass and ornaments — people
Applied effort and skill to create the
Cabinets and artwork but today I

Avoid looking at them — the debris in
My life has accumulated and needs
Careful attention — time and energy —
Patience and sorting through to discover

What's worth keeping — what should be discarded —
As most of what I have just collects dust.

Every decision
over everything
will be a rearrangement
and a paring down of
superfluity.

A home contains the habits of those who
Live within it and my cats every night
Would sleep in her room with her as I was
Left in blissful solitude — and as her

Absence is being felt with the days and
Weeks I've been watching the cats to see how
They would respond — when Henry who seldom
Attended to me looked in my eyes with

Inquiry as if to say — where is she —
When Kitcat wandered throughout the house while
Yowling as he was not in the habit
Of doing beforehand — though with Johnnie

I'm not observing any difference
But I'm not sure that means he doesn't care.

Henry and Johnnie
like to take the space in the
center of the bed
so I have to push them off —
Kitcat wanders in the night.

There is a chilly dampness about the
Air and the gray sky is imposing a
Somberness over the morning as I
Am driving and noticing the orange

And red scattered among the green leaves in
Stillwater — as I am absorbing yet
Another turning of the seasons with
A recycling of sights I've seen so

Many times before — accumulating
A weightiness and grandeur with the years
Knowing the orbits within the orbits
The earth and the sun are subject to — I

Feel the repetition and the impact
Of time incessantly recreating.

And yet there is a
poignancy about
these days about my
dissolving family which
is a new experience.

It's early in autumn but the robins
Have already left and are migrating
To sunnier landscapes a friend told me —
Also saying that robins migrate in

Flocks — which was news to me — it's easy not
To notice the absence of the robins
As they are a tiny detail of the
Air and the sky among the millions of

Cyclical changes in a season — I
Notice the robins singing at sunrise
And pecking at the earthworms in puddles
Collecting in my driveway after a

Soaking shower during the spring — but there
Are so many things to see in summer.

The robins aren't separate
from the air and sky
but are always a part of
the air and sky — even if
they're not here.

I'm hosting my subscribers and donors
To a dinner and speech at a fancy
Restaurant hoping to generate the
Donations necessary for success

Our speaker is an expert on healthcare
And two judges a senator and a
Mayor are attending — we oppose the
Tentacles of the bureaucratic state

Resisting the crushing octopus of
Mandates and regulations resulting
In waiting lists and rationing — we are
Intelligent and enthusiastic

And we share a belief in liberty
Which is weakening in America.

The magazine I
publish is laboring
against the tide of
dominating
opinion.

I could write continuous lines about
Economic and bureaucratic facts
Arguing what I believe is the most
Humane point of view — but regardless of

My intentions I'd only engender
Disagreement — and my offerings would
Not amount to poetry — arguments and
Bitterness and confusion are part of

Society — with coalitions of
People trying to get the better of
Other people — and yet companionship
And love and art and music are also

Part of society as we oscillate
Between belligerence and harmony.

I am part
rascal
part lover
depending on
viewpoints.

A prominent politician's son is
Placed on the board of directors of a
Foreign energy company while the
Politician is in position to

Influence the course of business — even
Though the son has no expertise
Or experience to qualify for
The job — the business prospers and the son

Reaps millions of dollars in a few years
While a trickle of information is
Reported — but the vitriol of a
Swarm of journalists is diverted from

The politician and the son onto
Those who are exposing the corruption.

The politician claims
to be a champion
for the little guy
and a crusader
against corruption.

Judging by the indifference of the
Nation's top media watchdogs to the
Evidence of the obvious pay for
Play dealings of government officials

Corruption and hypocrisy are part
Of the game — as long as the practice is
Artfully concealed — but America
Is thought to be different — we believe

In liberty and justice — both parties
Profess to champion the little guy —
To force the billionaires to pay fairly
For the upkeep of the unfortunate —

But even within the United States
The ruling class is protecting itself.

Playing with words
generates joy and
enthusiasm while
watching politics
makes me tired.

The Big Dipper appears in the Northern
Sky — near the horizon in fall and high
In summer — the pattern was discovered
To be a bear by tribal ancestors

In Canada who said every autumn
Warriors hunt the bear and the green leaves
Are spattered by the bloody wounds of the
Bear — the ancient Phoenicians mariners

Navigated by the Dipper stars — and
Astronomers say in twenty-five thousand
Years the Big Dipper will be similar —
Even though the stars are incessantly

Moving and each star is variously
Distant — and dozens of light years away.

The stars are expanding
the mountains and hills are
rising and falling
like the waves of a
cosmic ocean.

They keep their appointed rounds about the
City streets — beginning before the dawn —
Witnessing the rising sun — enduring
Blizzards in winter — rain in spring — sticky

Air in summer — directing such massive
Vehicles and marshaling hundreds of
Horsepower engines — projecting power —
Revving their engines up and down — starting

And stopping — I see them on the hilly
Streets of Stillwater — standing while they are
Driving their trucks — as if piloting a
Ocean-going vessel over rolling

Swells — I imagine they are flexible
By bending their knees — rising and falling.

Garbage truck drivers
are unappreciated heroes
directing such
mechanized marvels.

If the space inside of an atom is
Ninety-nine percent empty — and if
The distance from the nucleus of the
Atom to the outer orbits of the

Atom's whirling electrons defining
The atom's size is comparable to
The pitcher's mound and the outer expanse
Of a baseball stadium — then all the

Things appearing in the world are mostly
Empty and we might be able to say
The world is mostly an illusion — but
While driving across an intersection

I was — smacked — by another vehicle
And my car spun around in a circle.

The impact left
me dazed and with
difficulty I focused on
the other driver's
insurance card.

I was looking for a parking place in
Minneapolis while all the streets were
Congested — driving parallel and one
Block over from a busy avenue

And I don't recall before the impact
Whether I stopped and looked before crossing
The intersection — but because it is
My habit to do so I assume I

Stopped and looked — and he clobbered my rear tire
On the passenger side spinning my car
Two hundred eighty degrees around — the
Impact was an absorbing sensation

Unlike anything I've experienced
Overloading and befuddling me.

Liability is a
word insurance companies
toss about — but I believe
he was
speeding.

Onions are ambrosia to the tongue
Melting to almost nothing inside of
My crock-pot while suffusing the corn
The cauliflower broccoli beef and

Mushrooms with flavor — an onion is a
Symbol of life — layer over layer
And day after day or year after year
And at the center nothing left over

And though I am harried with things to do
And I am giving my energy to
The pivotal decisions — and I am
Neglecting my sensibilities — I

Hope the day will finally come when
I learn to be an adequate cook.

I learned the
French method for
cutting onions — don't
cut the halves the way through
to keep from fumbling.

Rain was falling sporadically through the
Afternoon but I needed to cut and
Bag the hostas and daylilies — so I
Wore a warm jacket hat and gloves and used

A hedge trimmer making easy work of
The yearly ritual marking a turn
Into winter — moving from plant to plant
Cutting raking bagging taking bags to

The street — attending only to simple
Activity taking somber pleasure
In the task pulling and bending with my
Arms and legs — my mind didn't wander much —

Overhead — mother-of-pearl sky — about
Me — trees were wearing their party colors.

In the soreness and
difficulty moving
my back and legs on
the morning afterwards
there is satisfaction.

Night is encroaching into daylight and
Shadow is obscuring the apple trees —
The brilliant light and gentle breezes are
Migrating with the formations of geese

Flying south — the windows are shut and the
Furnace is humming and I am wearing
Socks for warmth while walking on the floorboards
Of my home — but there is a radiance

Penetrating the overcast sky as
I can see that the gray clouds are glowing
As the memory of all the winter
Skies I've ever seen are so familiar

But a radiance is persisting and
Penetrating another cloudy day.

No matter how cold
and overcast the
day the sky will be
radiant with the
ever-present light.

Waves of light are very fast — waves of sound
Are slower — the pull and release of tides
Are reliable — the cycles of the
Moon and the rotation of the earth are

Constant — seasons are repetitive and
Yet the dispersion of the leaves and the
Withdrawal of warmth comes with shock that life
Is getting serious now — it's time to

Bundle up — the grass is green today but
The gray sky is portentous and it is
Much easier to imagine a spray
Of snow descending in a bitter wind —

How much of my life have I forgotten?
How am I choosing what to remember?

Light waving
moon cycling
winter returning
remembering
forgetting.

Wheeling the receptacle of trash to
The street on Thursday morning I noticed
A light on the driveway — looking for the
Source I saw the moon brightly looming in

The sky — not appearing orange and near
The horizon but high and luminous in
In the night — cool verging into cold air
Was uncomfortable enough to rouse me

To wakefulness and I imagined the
Chinese river and mountain poets who
Renounced the contentious ways of cities
Who lived alone surrounded by mountains —

They professed to celebrate solitude
By drinking wine and savoring moonshine.

Were they savoring
bare awareness or
just dulling the pain
of loneliness?

Chinese created grasslands and rivers —
They conceived the waterfalls thundering
Into ravines — they revealed the crags of
The cloud generating mountains that brought

Sunlight and distance to life — the needles
Of a single masterful pine are
Strangely evocative and the tiny
Figure dressed in rags relying on a

Staff crossing a rickety bridge spanning —
Emptiness — are all that is left behind
Of a life — leaving me to imagine
The sinuous motion of a brush and

Wrist tracing in single lines of flowing
Ink only the essential impressions.

Someone dedicated
so much of himself to
crafting sinuous lines
of ink tracing only
the barest outlines.

A part of me always rejoices with
The sight of red and orange leaves every
Autumn — maybe because of persisting
Memories I have of dressing up in

Colorful costumes for Halloween in
Childhood — because we made the changing
Of the seasons into winter festive by
By creating a ceremony to

Cover up the withdrawal of vibrancy
And the imminence of shadowy months —
But apart from ceremony — and in
Themselves — the autumn leaves are beautiful —

The scarlet and orange and yellow leaves
Remind me beauty is temporary.

And yet beauty
reappears
reliably
spontaneously.

Not only am I — depending on the my
Mood — seeing a distorted image of
Myself and of my place within the world —
As if I were a funhouse mirror — but

I consider how my acquaintances
And my friends see themselves and their places
Within the world and I discover how
Differently strangely and opposed to my

Way of thinking they really are — then I
Ask myself are all of us — depending
On our various moods — living in one
World or are we a baffled company

Milling through a hall of funhouse mirrors
And it's a wonder we communicate.

Usually I'm better off
listening more than speaking
because listening opens
my ears and allows
the fumes to escape.

I am not burdened by the drizzling rain
Because I don't have to shovel the rain
But in a couple of weeks or even
Days the precipitation will turn to

Snow and snow on the driveways and streets is
Hazardous if not removed — the window pane
Is streaked with the rills of rain on the verge
Of freezing distorting the view of my

Cottonwood — the cottonwood has dropped a
Scattered allotment of leaves but even
A boisterous wind cannot take the leaves from
The tree because the tree isn't ready —

Isn't finished drinking the sunshine yet
Isn't prepared for its unconsciousness.

All at once the yellow
leaves come down to
brighten the grass and
rapidly they become
brittle and brown.

In summer all the leaves up and down the
Cottonwood will flutter in a breeze and
Sparkle in the sunlight and it's easy
To imagine the leaves are bells pealing

Leafy music — perhaps in the darkness
Of the night and on an overcast day
The tree is resting and sipping as much
Of the sunlight and moonlight as it can —

As every leaf is a little tongue and
Always receptive — but over a week
In autumn there comes a time when the tree
Releases its leaves and becomes dormant —

My cottonwood is harmonious with
The revolutions of the earth and sun.

All the trees
release their leaves
when the time comes in
effortless harmony.

Maybe in the future technology
Will give birth to genetically enhanced
Human beings leveraging implanted
Computer chips focusing cognition

But today I am enjoying my new
Toyota Corolla — with leather seats
And a sunroof — interfacing with my
Phone enabling me to make calls while

My hands are guiding the steering wheel — while
Receiving voice and screen directions to
My destination as I maneuver
Using satellites orbiting the earth —

But what would happen if technology
Were applied as a tool of surveillance?

Technology tracking
driving patterns
communication
likes and dislikes
even thoughts?

When the leaves are blowing in the wind in
Swirls or one by one the bareness of the
Branches and the trunks are gradually
Revealed again for another winter

And the dissipation of the leaves in
Stillwater — depending on the timing
Of the differing trees — happens over
A couple of weeks — the brightness of the

Foliage precedes a stark nakedness and
The rustling of the wind in the leaves is
Noticeably absent — I am living
Alone in a house full of memories

And the dispersal of my family
This morning came as a revelation.

Stabs of
memory
reside in
household
items.

The snow blower's electric starter is
Not working and in November it takes
Wrenching excruciating exhausting
Pulls of the starter cord to make it go

The machine was getting worse every year
And on the occasion of the first snow
Last winter my pulling was quite futile —
My swearing made no difference at all —

In February the machine will start
With a single pull but in November
It's an obstacle I dread confronting
And I'm yanking on the cord in nightmares

So this year I borrowed the use of a
Friend's pickup truck and took it for repair.

The mechanic mumbled
something about
flushing the carburetor
changing spark plugs
too much oil in the gas.

Kitcat likes the dry food the other cats
Aren't allowed because of their aliments
And I feed him alone in my bedroom —
I serve his food within a Tupperware

Container and when he's done he pounds on
The door for me to let him out — and I
Let him out and lid the container and
Put it away so he can't knock it off

The counter — as he often does just so
He can seize my attention — but today
As soon as I let him out and lidded
The container he was looking for the

Container to knock it off the counter
And he was yowling to be fed again.

I thought women were
tricky but Kitcat with
a brain the size of a
walnut is bossing
me around.

When the trees have dispersed their leaves again
When seeing through the bare branches again
Comes as a shock on a frosty morning —
Then the sunrise on the horizon is

Brilliant — as the touches of yellow and
Orange and pink spread along a distant
Line and shine in a predominately
Drab landscape — and when the sun emerges

On the horizon the light seems to rise
From the frosty grass revealing again
The subdued greens of the shrubs and pines — then
The motion of the cars reverberates

Along the streets and between the homes of
Stillwater — echoing in the quiet.

I notice the
necessity for
gloves and boots and
fabric to wrap
around my neck.

The weight of an overcast sky can be
Oppressive and ominous of coming
Burdens when the seasons turn to winter
Again when the bare branches suddenly

Take on a skeletal appearance — in
November the cold arises with a
Shock despite repeated experience —
Like being dunked into freezing water —

But I am noticing the covering
Sky in another light giving the sun
Due appreciation for persistence
And for the penetration of daylight —

Even when the snow is descending in
Overwhelming flakes the sun is present.

An overcast sky
even the cascading
snowflakes are
suffused and glowing
with sunlight.

His ears are enormous extending out
From his head and appearing sensitive
And capable of absorbing whispers —
His nose and nostrils are exorbitant

His chin and teeth are prominent — and with
The large dark pools of his eyes he gazes
About steadily and peacefully and then
Suddenly he can become excited —

He is sloped-shouldered and elongated
And his neck and legs are especially
Exaggerated in length and when he
Moves he ambles and lopes in swinging strides

Rhythmically and lackadaisically
And yet he covers the ground quite quickly.

The
muscular
tongue
can
grab
leaves
but
why
does
the
giraffe
have
two
horns?

There are so many details hanging in
The air without worthy explanation
And I have often lain awake at night
Wondering why do the giraffes have tails

Because in proportion to their bodies
This little protuberance wouldn't serve
As much protection as a fly swatter
Except the to sensitive puckering

Directly under the tail — and the tuft
Would be quite unnecessary for that —
Perhaps in the compilation of the
Organism the flicking or swishing

Instrument is useful for expression
Or maybe it's only an afterthought?

A
quizzical
swish
or
a
petulant
flick
could
be
quite
communicative.

If lawyers had tails they would exercise
Caution and discipline in the courtroom
Not to flicker nervously about but
To swish with confidence and rectitude

When upon their hind legs questioning a
Witness or presenting evidence — and
They would eliminate superfluous
Gesturing including the wayward tips

Practicing a curl of dignity or
An upright pose of sobriety while
Leaving for the closing arguments the
Dramatically vigorous sweep and snap

Or imagine the declamatory
Righteousness of unwavering tautness.

Out of
court
lawyers
with tails
could
afford
to
be
limp
and
list-
less.

The days between my disposal of the
Cottonwood leaves and blizzards are blissful
Because I don't have to do anything
Outside and the wind may howl in the trees

And the temperature may plummet but
I'm prepared with winter fleeces mittens
Boots and berets — and the warmest blankets —
The furnace is humming the curtains are

Drawn against the early evening darkness
And the car is safe within the garage —
Preparing for snow is a ritual
Repeated year after year becoming

A somber celebration once the work
Is finished harvesting satisfaction.

On some years the ground
stays bare of snow until
Christmas and I'm fooled
thinking this will be
an easy winter.

When remembering previous winters
It is easy to be casual in
Conversation recalling a storm in
March or a snowfall in November or

The few days in January when we
Seemed to be having a surprising spring
Followed of course by a blasting of cold
And a battering of blizzards with the

Snow accumulating in piles along
Streets and driveways higher than me because
I was freezing my fingers pushing a
Snow blower and scraping with a shovel —

Winter in Minnesota becomes a
Nonsensical trudging in the tundra.

I am a
survivor with
post traumatic
February
disorder.

The apple trees
and lilac bushes
bloom together in spring
and hold their leaves
past the first snowfall.

— *Tekkan*

Everyday Mind XIII

We turn our clocks
an hour backwards
on November 3rd
but regardless
the darkness lengthens.

Compassion was boring he said and if
People would leave him alone everything
Would be o-ke-do-ke but if someone
Were so careless as to cross his path as

If they were a delinquent slinky
At the top of a flight of steps he would
Topple them over and gleefully watch them
Tumble down the stairs — but that was many

Years ago — before he found a seat with
The circles of sober alcoholics
And now he displays a generous and
Warm curmudgeoncy and he practices

A sharp and antiseptic honesty
Finagling somehow to become happy.

He is grateful
sobriety allows
him to enjoy his
grandchildren.

A mist is occupying Stillwater
This morning obscuring the homes and trees
While clearing a little in these minutes
With outlines becoming visible

As it seems an overbearing winter
Sky is descending from its lofty height
Settling on the earth as a moist layer
Of overnight snow is melting on the

Grass making it easy to believe that
There are no separate things and events
As the not quite freezing air and sky are
Saturating my consciousness with the

Expectation of much colder days and
The satisfaction of being prepared.

The snow is melting
on the metal of the
shovel as I'm moving
my legs and scraping
the driveway.

The sky is snow white again this morning
As white as yesterday although today
It has resumed its accustomed height and
The trees are making a leafless and a

Tangled outline underneath the looming
Sky as the air is warmer and the snow
Has vanished as if it were only a
Fantasy while the grass and the bushes

Are sprinkled with drops of water as all
The winters I remember are hinting
That these predominately cloudy days
Are here for the duration almost as

If a lid were slipped over the earth and
A covering will remain until spring.

The details
are predictable
yet somehow they
surprise.

Our group was removing the cushions from
The chapel and returning them to the
Cabinet down the corridor as we
Were chatting happily as usual

After meditation with everyone
Putting away the bells and the altar
And returning the chairs to their places
Inside the chapel amidst the hubbub

Of happy bantering conversation
Mixing activity with blather as
I was trimming the candle that needed an
Expenditure of effort because it's

Been neglected with me pulling the knife
Towards me while my thinking was aflutter.

Slicing my knuckle
open reminded me
of the simplicity of
doing one thing
at a time.

My instructions on driving motorbikes
Informed me not to fixate on potholes
Because doing so would guarantee my
Hitting the pothole because the bike goes

Exactly where I'm looking so I learned
To cast my sight strategically to lean
Into a curve and most of all to be
Alert but these days I'm writing about

Politics and following the news and
Watching deceitful personalities
And fabricated incendiary
Narratives and even if I'm alert

It's hard to absorb the psychodrama
Without becoming somewhat cynical.

Wearing a helmet
while reading news
isn't helpful.

I use an electric clipper only
To trim the pesky hair that sprouts under
My nostrils because the razor is quite
Impossible to maneuver there and

I hate looking in the mirror on the
Inside of the sun visor of my car
And seeing several egregious bristles
But sometimes when I push the switch to start

The clipper nothing happens and swearing
Doesn't help so I drop the clipper on
The countertop repeatedly until
For some mysterious reason it works —

It's absolutely necessary to
Jar the clipper so much to make it start.

I'm not sure
refinement
is a fair
description
of my life.

I get invested emotionally
In what I write and after polishing
A poem I print and place it inside
A briefcase and leave it until evening

And the lapse of hours occupied with
Other activity separates me
From my jewel so when reading it again
Sometimes I gain the clarity to see

Egregious errors but when the time comes
To edit a hundred poems at once
Initially I'm repulsed and ashamed
Because reading them is like looking in

A mirror and becoming engrossed with
My mannerisms stripped of delusions.

I need to persevere
to reconnect with
the original
inspiration.

Zen masters will question — who are you — and
Offering your name or profession or
Your status within society aren't
The answers to satisfy them as they

Will ask who is looking through your eyes what was
Your original face your face before
Conception what is the true color of
Your heart why is your hand so much like the

Buddha's hand and they will assert that you
Do not exist and you cannot seize the
Answers by anything you do or by
Anything you don't do while your thinking

Isn't helpful and not thinking isn't
Much better because you can't stop thinking.

A *hintergeanken*
is a suspicion
of something
that can't be
admitted.

We have had our baptismal snowfall of
The season and as is typical of
The beginning when the temperature
Hovers about freezing the snow was wet

And heavy and the morning afterwards
The sticky snow is adhering to the
Trunks and the bare branches of the trees and
Giving to Stillwater a fantasy

Frosted candy land appearance but the
Chill of the snow is sobering the white
Sky is ominous and the chunky piles
Of snow the city plows have left along

The street are reminding me of twenty
Years of dragging winter experience.

Atop the asphalt
of my driveway
the thinnest layer of
ice demarks where
the rain became the snow.

We gather within the spacious and
Windowed atrium of a church we one
Hundred sixty sober alcoholics
As we do every year celebrating

Our sobriety on Thanks Giving Day
Each of us taking a turn saying our
Names and briefly reciting why we are
Grateful while everyone is listening

And it's always a happy occasion
Greeting companions again we haven't
Seen for a year reacquainting ourselves
Enjoying conversation preceding

And following our seated statements as
The room reverberates with our chatter.

Imagine the havoc
one hundred sixty
active drug addicts
and alcoholics
would be.

While I was visiting a temple in
Japan focusing myself with intense
Meditation newspapers would publish
Artwork presenting images of grass

Or of tulips and within the tulips
Or the grass outlines of a duck or of
A cat would be concealed but to see the
Duck or the cat I would have to squint my

Eyes just so as the optical trick was
Finagled with tiny dots upon a
Cheap quality of paper and sometimes
I could see the duck within the tulips

And sometimes I couldn't so I wondered
Is this another way of doing Zen?

A grim and
experienced monk
wasn't amused
by my question.

Soggy snow will make a slushy noise if
You toss a shovelful in the air and
Listen to it settle on a pile but
I don't spare the time for frivolity

When clearing driveways as it's too much work
And the snow blower is useless getting
Clogged as it does so I stab the shovel
Into the snow and onto the asphalt

And become a plow by keeping my legs
Moving pushing and pushing and pushing
And I'm bundled for the exercise with
Only two points of weakness which are my

Thumbs even when it's not too cold because
Even in mittens they are outstanding.

My toes are snug
inside my moonboots
but thumbs are
vulnerable to the
burning cold.

They hardly seem like anything falling
Constantly all morning and into the
Afternoon as the tiniest snowflakes
Steadily dropping from beyond the bare

Branches falling from a white sky distant
But impossible to gage the distance
Because there's nothing to compare it with
Beyond the bare branches only seeing

The white sky is inseparable from
The descent of the puniest of the
White snowflakes accumulating in the
Morning and throughout the afternoon and

Once I cleared the driveway and saw the black
Of the asphalt but now it's overcome.

White sky
and snowflakes
are sticking to
the bare branches.

In the dark hours before dawn sometimes I
Wake and then my thinking refuses to
Sleep and so there is the choice of whether
To lie in bed and passively review

My difficulties or to rise and dress
And sit before a computer screen with
My fingers poised and tapping out my thoughts
As they arise even though there's nothing

Special to discover and the thinking
Shapes itself around how the words will
Fit together and whether a flow of
Ideas and rhythm emerges and

Maybe a pursuit of something worthy
Of the effort of expression will come.

It's often a race
whether I reach a
destination before
dawn or I'm overcome
with drowsiness.

Stillwater

Regardless of the weather my comings
And goings lead me almost every day
To a view of the broad river with its
Valley southwards while the sun is rising

And I also see the ornate mansions
Built during the era of the lumber
Barons with the harvested timber of
The time located atop the bluffs of

The city — usually I hurry
On my way but when the sun is shining
Reflecting off the river and glinting from
The windows of the mansions on the bluffs

I'm struck by the beauty of Stillwater —
The limestone the valley and the river.

The Crossing Bridge
three miles away
a mile across
gracefully spans
the distance.

The refraction of yellow and blue and
White that I see when looking downriver
At the sunlight on the water and the
Snowy banks of the valley are waves of

Light bouncing off the river and valley
And into my eyes where electrical
Impulses are creating a spectrum
Of color in gradients of detail

And when my friend says — isn't this morning
Beautiful — waves of sound are entering
My ears and creating a question and
Prompting an instantaneous response —

Yes it really is a beautiful day
After so many gloomy snowy days.

My head is
awash in
cosmic waves
creating
emotions.

If only I had a formidable
Horn protruding from the center of my
Forehead I would be presenting a most
Imposing appearance as a force to

Be wary of and of course it wouldn't
Do to support a warrior's armament
With a slack jawed slope-shouldered comportment —
I'd have to have a barrel chest and stout

Legs well apart and firmly placed upon
The earth and I would have to assume an
Uncompromising and a humorless
Attitude without sensitivity

Or subtlety because otherwise what
Would be the point of possessing the horn?

Who ever
heard of a
fastidious
or simpering
rhinoceros?

Only by looking in a mirror can
I assess the features of my face and
Thereby compare myself with others to
Play the game of identity based on

Comeliness or the lack of comeliness
And it seems so simple not to play the
Game — don't look and don't care — but not caring
Is hard to do while even a mirror

Is limited as it cannot reveal
To me the inside of my head behind
My eyes — how does the inside of my head
Look — is there something or nothing there to

See and yet my eyesight captures so much
Of the evanescing panorama.

There is no mirror
between the world and
me except the image of
me I interpose.

Rohatsu

Pain in the legs and back is expected
When doing repeated periods of
Meditation and it's continuous
And coincident with the arising

Of energy and it takes vigorous
Effort to stay in the lotus posture
Though the night of starting and ending bells
Seeing in the dim electric light the

Shadow of my unmoving seated form
Extending before me on the carpet —
The slow and careful placing of our feet
As we pace the minutes out in silence

Walking in a circle as we do does
Relieve the intensity of sitting.

Burning
like a
candle
through the
night.

The familiar neighborhood is transformed
By the descending snowflakes as I can
See the homes the bare trees the spiky pines
Obscurely through the snow as the specks of

Falling whiteness are everywhere as I
Left my car in the garage thinking it's
Better not to worry about getting
Stuck within the accumulation on

The streets walking to the office in my
Boots holding a thermos of coffee in
Each mitten I trudge along wondering
How can the sky be distinguished from the

Snow and realizing the snow a while
Ago was a swelling and rolling ocean.

Tiny flakes
touch my
face and
inform
me of
the cold.

If I were to remark there is no time
And that there isn't any distance and
Also that there aren't separate events
You may think that I am nonsensical

But in nature seconds and minutes and
Hours do not exist apart from human
Fabrication and the idea of
Infinity is a phantom of the

Mind — also I cannot pick up an inch
From the ground and the miles I amble in
Summer from my home to the Crossing Bridge
Over the river and back to my home

On the north hill is just manner of
Measuring what I can do with my feet.

The swelling ocean
evaporating water
drifting clouds
and snow are
continuous.

When it's cold outside I use a trick to
Make things easier by opening the
Outside door and inserting the key while
Standing in the warmth inside the home so

I don't have to stand outside fumbling
With my bare hands in the cold because my
Mittens are too thick to be able to
Handle locking the door and of course I

Dress in layers of clothes as if I were
Weaving a chrysalis about me and
It's a pleasurable moment in the
Day when getting out of bed that I can

Insert my barest feet into the most
Luxurious and fuzziest of socks.

The foundation of
the coldest of days
is a warm and
comfy pair of
socks.

Holiday Poem

If I were much more weighty than I am
It would be fun lumbering into a
Room and striding slowly without any
Wiggly toes and swishing my meager

Tail and flapping my exorbitant ears
Using my demeanor to demonstrate
My excitement and my intention to
Exact a moment of retribution

And I might even pause for a while to
Allow my enormous presence in the
Tiny room to exert authority
And then I would trumpet my voice about

And then with intensity of purpose
I would seize on the rascal with my trunk.

I would use my
elephant's weight
to sit upon and
squash the pesky
relative.

I make an effort not to be fooled by
Events into believing that I am
Unworthy when I am discouraged or
That I am superior when things are

Going well because I think the cosmos
Is an unceasing emanation of
Waves more than light and sound but also my
Perceptions and responses come in waves

And I cannot wrench myself into a
Happy undulation when in a trough
And I'm making an effort to recall
There cannot be a crest without a trough —

To be a floating jellyfish or a
Masterful surfer — that is the question.

A reactive
and resentful
jellyfish doesn't
recognize
waves.

Poor Henry who has kidney disease is
Looking up at me from the floor with
A steady gaze intending I think to
Express something but it's hard knowing what

He wants as he's been fed and I'm happy
To observe that he's been eating almost
Normally although in quite small portions
And when he's looking at me in this way

It usually does mean he's hungry so
I do feed him because the disease will
Make him constipated which causes him
Not to eat so when he wants to eat I

Seize the opportunity to give him
The food he needs to live a little more.

Henry is a cat
with a penetrating
gaze but I don't know
what he's trying to say.

Henry makes a raspy disgruntled growl
Johnnie whines incessantly for his food
Kitcat is an adolescent fool who
Takes a rascal's pleasure in wrestling

And biting the smaller cats about their
Necks and Kitcat pushes items off the
Kitchen counter seizing my attention
But I am dominating by turning

Doorknobs and opening the tins of food —
Sometimes I am serious with Kitcat
Staring at him with dissatisfaction
Pronouncing nonsensical noises and

Looming over him and raising a hand
While he rolls on his back wanting to play.

I go about the
house singing to
the cats and they
don't take me
seriously.

Humans are funny animals who can
Acquire a supplementary skin
Through cleverness and selection and I
Fashion for myself a layer of warmth

And comfort in the winter by wearing
Garments composed of synthetic fiber
Called polar fleeces countering the drab
Landscape consisting of longer nights and

Frozen air and the perpetual brown
Of the trees and the white of the snow I
Am wearing the brightest orange and red
And green and the bluest blue bell of blue

And my vulnerable wiggly toes
Are swaddled in the warmest fuzzy socks.

Cat hair sticks to
the polar fleeces
and I find myself
perpetually
picking off the hairs.

People may suppose that managing a
Political movement is all about
Promoting a system of ideals
But in modern America the trick

Consists in persuading mass numbers of
Voters to hate the right sort of people
As the whole operation depends on
Directing attention away from the

Mismanagement and the thievery that
Politicos are engaged in because
The American middle class always
Produces the most stupendous pile of

Taxpayer's money in the history
Of the world and the money is the prize.

Great white sharks constantly
swim to prevent drowning —
politicos accuse others
of doing what they
do.

I listen to politicos and know
They can't possibility believe what they are
Saying and they overlook the fact that
Their words are on video and when at

Different times because of altering
Circumstances they take exactly the
Opposite sides of the same issue — all
The while professing utter sincerity —

They seem unconcerned that such audacious
Shameless hypocrisy is obvious
To anyone paying attention but
They rely on the ignorance and the

Fickleness of public opinion and
On a sympathetic media.

They are brazen
because of the
overabundance
of anger and
ignorance.

There are blue skies in every season but
When the snow is accumulated on
The ground and when the air is freezing then
As the sun rises on the horizon

And illuminates the river valley
The sun is a glowing brilliant disk of
Orange lighting the graceful cables of
The Crossing Bridge in the distance and

Shining everywhere on the snow on the
Ground and I can see the sparkle of the
Sun refracted in the pinpoint jewels of
Blue and green and red appearing as if

The snow were a magical blanket and
Winter is worthy of celebration.

So often during winter
it seems as though
an overcast lid were
stretched over the sky.

Words as I compose them on a screen by
Paying attention to their rhythms and
Sounds and meanings by training myself to
Seize on whatever is piquant today —

Believing as I do there is always
Something worthy of celebration in
A day — allow me to forget about
My troubles for an hour and the hunt for

And discovery of the perfect fit for
The exact word is so pleasurable
That satisfaction suffuses my days
And difficulties that would otherwise

Sap my energy and discourage me
Will seem no more than a passing trifle.

The act of
spontaneously
choosing
a word
is joyous.

However do the trees survive through the
Winter when the ground is frozen and their
Roots are inert and the tips of their twigs
Are leafless and all they can do is to

Stand in the wind and create a howling —
And however does my heart beat itself
And my lungs breathe themselves as if they were
Disconnected from whatever concern

Is presently occupying my mind —
And are these happenings similar to
Or the same as the energy causing
The sun to burn itself — and the stars of

The Milky Way to burn themselves as they
Are revolving around a massive hole?

The thinnest of clouds
are moving across
the sky unhindered
by any thought of
needing to perform.

I am resolving today to dispose
Of the things that are cluttering my life
As just a glance around my office desk
Reveals the many business cards that I

Have no memory of collecting and
There is the Christmas card from a person
I barely knew who died years ago and
Perhaps I decided to keep the card

Because he was an artist and sent a
Drawing of Dayton Ohio where he
Lived showing the skyline of the city
Maybe on a sunny afternoon when

He traced his city in graceful lines and
Now I am reluctant to part with it.

There is a tug
to hang on to
little parcels of
memory.

I am a natural meditator
As the sand in the desert is too hot
To swivel within during the day and
Inactivity conserves energy

For my hunting in the night when the grains
Of the sand are cooled and continuous
Motion is easier than thinking and
Sashaying and waiting and flicking my

Tongue are exciting as I determine
Where to go depending on which of the
Forks of my tongue will taste the tang of a
Scent for undulation and waiting and

Flicking and watching and coiling about
For an impulsive application of fangs.

Vibrating
fear
anger
danger
makes
me
rattle.

Living alone for the first time during
Christmas and New Year's Day for me is a
Different rhythm as the house needs a
Cleaning and in the process of wiping

Dust off the piano and of throwing
Out containers of unused food and of
Scrubbing every surface and corner of
The refrigerator while listening

To music I am quite surprisingly
Generating enthusiasm while
Accidentally I nudge the cuckoo
Clock and hear the familiar ticking

I haven't heard for many years as the
House is beginning to be a home again.

The clock was
dusty and idle
because my ex-wife
disliked the
cuckooing.

When working for the Andersen Windows
Corporation Jim merged his body with
The mechanical repetition of
Assembling windows for a number

Of hours a day but in retirement
He gives his attention to the sky and
The trees to rivers and lakes in a hunt
For the miraculous revelation

Of birds — he told me why the house sparrows
Were brought from England and released into
The parks of New York City — to eat the
Moth larvae ravaging the trees and now

The sparrows have spread everywhere killing
The butterflies native birds and flowers.

Jim sees the wood ducks
blue-winged teals
trumpeter swans
prairie warblers
painted redstarts.

I don't know the differences between a
Finch and a yellow-bellied sapsucker
And the only bird I see every day
Is a bird requiring no special

Knowledge or talent to identify —
The somber crow impervious to the
Hardships of winter — but Jim possesses
The sensibility to admire the

Variety and elegance of birds
And by virtue of his passion insight
Animates him and the air and the trees
The river valley and Stillwater's bluffs

Are full of evanescent loveliness
On the fly and seen only in moments.

What a gift it is
to be on the hunt
searching the air
for just a glimpse
of beauty.

I remember an hour before dawn
In Kyoto thirty years ago that
Was such a lovely departure from the
Consistently sweltering summer air

When the window was open and rain was
Pattering on a walkway outside and
I can hear the sound of the rain again
Recall the luscious coolness of the air

When I wrapped myself within a blanket
Savoring swaddling warmth in the dark
While the bamboo was knocking together
And rain was spattering on the concrete —

Whatever worries I carried then are
Forgotten but I remember the rain.

I remember the
throbbing of cicadas
through a summer haze
while looking over Kyoto
from the eastward mountains.

Why do I remember some things and not
Others and who does the remembering
Because I'm not quite the assemblage
Of propensities that I was and yet

Some experience is echoing through
The decades as I have applied myself
To accumulate a compendium
Of knowledge and skills and usually

In circumstances my actions are a
Repetition of my past behavior
And I don't think much about responding
But in conversation with family

Sometimes I discover we have said things
Or been to places I have forgotten.

Perhaps I'm like a
whirlpool in a river
swirling and forgetting
as much as remembering.

It doesn't matter whether I'm in the
Mood to write because when I arrive at
My desk while the sun is rising I am
Alert and able to leverage my

Thinking and whether the rippling of
My mind is rehearsing the reasons why
I should be angry or I am blaming
People because I'm lonely and they don't

Care or whether I'm happy and the sun
Is resplendent — it doesn't matter if
I'm moody — because I love weighing the
Meaning of words and searching for just the

Right angle to communicate with you
And whatever I was feeling is gone.

Please understand
my poems employ
turning words which
emanate
satisfaction.

Christmas is done — New Year's Eve is coming —
Soon the seasonal landmarks will have passed
And I have a habit of taking out
My binoculars and seeing onto

Spring on the far horizon where lilac
Bushes and cherry and apple trees are
Blossoming but between here and there is
A long weary trudge through the tundra of

Winter and I know from experience
That into March and April and even
May there are teasing intervals when it
Seems that winter is finally finished

And yet an arctic front descends on us
With abominable wet heavy snow.

It's better to
put the binoculars
away and appreciate
that every snowflake is
unique.

I am the only person in my home
With the ability to open doors
And tins of food while I am surrounded
By personalities mischievous

Whiny and grumpy — when I'd like to sleep
Just a little longer in the morning
There's a pounding on my door summoning
Me to the kitchen to open the tins

Of food — though I've become proficient at
Ignoring noises — and whenever I
Am at home I can depend on my cats
For the fellowship a lonely guy needs —

They don't impose themselves excessively
They are less temperamental than people.

Henry is wasting away
with kidney disease and
at some point I'll need
to determine when
to put him under.

We had a conversation this morning
On the occasion of New Year's Day and
We sober alcoholics discussed the
Endeavor of living free from the snares

Of unkind thoughts and bitterness and free
Of every fear of the future and we
Would like to be liberated from our
Gloom despondency and disappointments

Because you see in our isolation
The world appears as a hall of funhouse
Mirrors showing a repetition of
Distorted images but when talking

To each other the hall of mirrors is
Dissolved and we see the world as it is.

Companionship and
communication
break down barriers
and we find ourselves
liberated.

I love the attention that comes to me
When I am able to express myself
And be understood — I love having the
Company of a companion able

To express her experience of the
Ephemeral world from a point of view
I could never have come to on my own
Because I am a drop of consciousness

Within an ocean of consciousness and
By myself I am incomplete tending
To dark meditations and I don't need
An affirmation of my opinions

I just love an exploration of our
Differing and complimentary views.

The unborn
undying
world is
beyond
knowing.

I am inclined to be apart from group
Opinion while not being overtly so
Because I recognize the power of
Mass hypnosis and sometimes I do doubt

Whether my view is accurate so I
Watch and play to my strength consisting
Of an underlying intuition
Despite the presence of ubiquitous

Controversy and chaos that things are
OK as they are determining me
To do what I can to be active and
Kind and optimistic with the people

I meet because my sphere of influence
Surpasses the extent of my knowledge.

This is an unceasing
and wounding cosmos
compelling me to
seek healing and
strength.

I brushed his hair for a final time and
Picked him up facing him to Johnnie and
Kitcat urging them to say goodbye and
To avoid inducing stress I put him

Into the carrier backwards so he
Couldn't see what I was doing until
He was inside — he was free to sniff and
Wander about the room until the vet

Removed him for a few minutes so she
Could insert the catheters into his
Veins — I held him in my lap — the vet pushed
The plungers of the syringes — pumped the

Drugs inside of him and so suddenly
He collapsed in my hands and departed.

Henry was a white cat
with orange spots and the
tips of ears were frozen
off in a winter before
he was recued years ago.

They were not large enough to wield a
Rifle or to thrust a bayonet in
Anger but the teenage drummer boys of
The Civil War communicated the

Commands of generals amidst the noise
Of battle with dozens of cadences
Signaling when to rally where to meet
When to attack and retreat — and they served

In field hospitals — but when the dispersed
Drummers on the field initiated
The steady beating of the long roll the
Soldiers were summoned in serried ranks

To master a terrible contest of
Minnie balls cannon balls and bayonets.

Drummers beat the
single and double drags
double stroke roll
flamadiddles
paradiddles
ratamacues
flam accents
flamacues
sextuplets
and ruffs.

On a clear morning in January
With snow on the ground and a chill in the
Wind my cottonwood is bathed in the light
Of the rising sun and the multitude

Of its limbs and twigs the entirety
Of its unsymmetrical sprouting so
High into the air is revealed in
The orange light of a rising sun in

Winter — every deep groove of its bark and
The remotest twig at the end of a
Crooked branch is visible and apart
From any abstract notion I conceive

Of what constitutes beauty as its quiet
Slumbering transcends my valuations.

On the corner of my
property by the fire
hydrant it is standing
appearing in all its
unexplainable presence.

It's easy to adopt a pattern of
Behavior repeatedly every day
Not noticing the ephemeral turn
Of events but I am seeing the sun

Rising on a couple of days in a clear
Sky over the drab landscape of winter
With a brilliant orange light and I am
Noticing the slanting of the sunrise

Lighting trees in the neighborhood for just
Several minutes of the day when the
Trees are reflecting the same resplendent
Orange as the sun while the houses and

The streets are not — as the sun caresses
The trees for a moment and passes on.

The chill of winter
reaches even inside
a heated home and
warm socks are a
necessity.

My alarm rings at 4:40 a.m.
And usually I'm able to leave
My bed and take care of my three felines —
Until last week — every morning my cats

Anticipate me watching and waiting
To be brushed and fed as I launch into
Nonsensical banter and song because
Whatever my cats derive from me has

Nothing to do with the meaning of words
But the joy and enthusiasm I
Generate does communicate and my
Little friends appreciate rituals

I believe as I learn an important
Lesson — I don't have to be serious.

Now that Henry's passed away
I'm discovering an
extra 10 minutes of
free time but I'd
rather have Henry.

My cats do not pretend to be happy
When they are obstinately annoyed
And I can grab Kitcat by the scruff of
His neck or knead the fur of his forehead

With my fingers or toss him on his back
And aggressively tickle his tummy
And he demonstrates his enjoyment by
Pursuing me after I walk away —

His intentions are clear when he's whining
For his food which is a habit he learned
From Johnnie — but people may be smiling
With their eyes and face while truly they are

Differing bored and not listening and
I might as well be talking to a wall.

Generally I am
optimistic and
enthusiastic but
it's hard for me to
smile for a photo.

I'm in a predicament because I
Know I need to be happy in photos
But the more determined I become to
Smile the more difficulty I'm having —

People are urging me to summon a
Lighthearted memory and a joyful
Expression will naturally blossom —
I don't doubt the effectiveness of the

Suggestion — I am sure it works for them —
They have pushed me in a good direction
And I'm resolved to follow their advice
But presently the harder I try the

Less likely I am to smile so perhaps
For now I will be happy with a grin.

Being
perfectly
purposely
spontaneous is
tricky.

It hasn't snowed for a week and the snow
On the ground is crusty on top and though
There isn't much wind when the slightest whiff
Touches the exposed skin on my face as

I'm moving from my car to the coffee
Shop I'm alerted instantly it is
Cold — I remember seeing the first drops
Of a summer rain striking the concrete

Before me on a Saturday in June
Thinking these are very large raindrops — then
I was plunked on my forehead — but today
It's necessary to be wary of

The ice on the walkway as a moment's
Inattention could result in a fall.

As I'm walking the
folds of my jeans are
communicating
the biting cold of
January.

The cold lingers upon the skin after
Entering a heated home for moments
Reminding me of what the cold is as
Nothing else could do and then I hear the

Whoosh of the furnace and the hum of the
Aquarium and the printer and I
Close my eyes listening allowing my
Ears to absorb the waves of sound throbbing

Within the room and there is the pulsing
Of my blood and the beating of my heart
But try as I might I can't do without
My eyes and outside the window beyond

A fringe of bare branches a thin layer
Of clouds very high up is hovering.

Bare awareness
is so much more
peaceful than the
fretful hassle of
thinking.

Our conversations have had an impact
As I've had the opportunity to
Hear about your experience and
Concerns and to see with your vision how

The world is manifesting — I'm trying
To decipher the explicit and the
Unspoken messages we have exchanged —
I'm attending to a tide within me

Attempting to surf my emotions and
Aspiring to poise and nimbleness
Knowing that I need to be in the flow
Surrendering expectations aiming

To be as light as a feather with you
And allowing the waves to carry me.

I'll paddle my
surfboard out
anticipating.

There are some movies that I love to watch
Because I am enchanted with the play
Of emotions on display — I like the
Antagonism of an oppressive

Society with stylish mendacity
When devils are perversely attractive —
The dynamic of rebellion against
Overwhelming odds overburdens a

Woman and a man creating a sense
Of mission compelling sacrifice and
Courage and every tremulous motion
Of their faces touches indecision and

Resolve — scorn and hatred — apprehension
And love — and the emotions resonate.

But when actors
venture political
opinions on current
issues their sanctimony
reverberates.

I know better than to come to my desk
With the intention of writing while my
Thinking is persistently distracted
And the effort assumes the aspect of

A tug of war with part of me striving
To enunciate ethereal words
While the rest of me is occupied with
Visceral urges as yesterday I

Signed up with a dating site and composed
A profile and uploaded my photos
And now I can't seem to keep myself from
Grasping for my phone anticipating

A bouncing bodacious and beautiful
Woman with a blossoming of welcome.

Whatever
ethereal words
might have come
are entirely
consumed.

To be alone with my thoughts and have no
Other perspective to balance mine would
Be an impoverishment of spirit
Because companionship far surpasses

The intellect as we communicate
So much of affection and harmony
With an attitude and gesture of the
Body in unguarded moments even

The slightest emotion flickers between
Us through our eyes and faces transforming
A tedious afternoon into an
Oasis that doesn't depend upon

Opinion but does bespeak a happy
Exploration of what life could become.

Difference is a
spice of intriguing
possibility.

It's almost a shame to sprinkle letters
And words across the pristine whiteness of
A page but if I didn't how could my
Playful exploration ever emerge —

I imagine emptiness to be black
With nothing inside of it and the black
Letters sprawling in serried lines upon
A page could be a frightful tickling

But the lovely and shapely appearance
Of my letters skipping along the page
May serve as a brave assertion of my
Frolic in the face of oblivion

But how could emptiness be black or white
And how does life and color emanate?

A bare tree under
a white sky in
January is a wilder
version of my
poem.

It is easy to become lost in thought
Thinking it's important to grasp the right
Ideology and the correct point
Of view but it is an inspiration

To ponder what was my original
Face and who was I before being born —
Am I more akin to the line of the
Horizon in the distance? To the clouds

Drifting in the sky? To the up-thrusting
Of a mountain weathering and slowly
Eroding? While it's true I do possess
Ideas and ideas do possess

Me doesn't being encompass so much
More than the categories of a mind?

Am I also the
burning sphere
of rock becoming
the earth with
breathable air?

I'll send a text and leave a message on
Your machine doing my business for the
Morning while waiting for a response and
Checking my phone in my pocket again

Anticipating your voice desiring
A connection imagining what you
May sound like as we haven't spoken yet
But there are the words we've exchanged and I

Have your profile on the website as you've
Brought me along setting the time and day
For our meeting asking me to choose the
Locale and I asserted Quixotic

Coffee yesterday and tomorrow is
Coming quickly but you haven't said yes.

Your figure is so
curvy in places
stimulating me
to extend myself
anticipating.

At about 4 a.m. if I leave my door
Open Johnnie comes in and begins to
Gnaw on a leg of the marble top stand
With his teeth because he knows doing that

Bothers me and I will say — stop it — and
When he keeps gnawing I will rise from bed
And toss him out of the room and close the
Door — then Kitcat pounces on Johnnie

Overwhelming him and then Johnnie yowls
And I rise from bed again and open
The door saying — shush — which they do for a
While but then the ruckus starts again while

I am determined not to get up so
Early but it's impossible to sleep.

My cats are determined that
I should feed them
at 4 a.m. — but I
won't — not until
4:40.

Even though it's not written into our
Laws and people do their business without
Being aware of its power it's hard
To deny the contention between us

Of a hierarchy of dominance
Whereby we sort ourselves in levels of
Status and influence involving the
Recognition of a thousand telltale

Signals of beauty intelligence and
Ability and I need to give
Biology respect but I rely
For comfort on spiritual jujitsu —

If I can be playful in my thinking
I will have the companionship I need.

There is enough
novelty and love
to go around.

From day to day it's easy to forget
The line of the horizon in the distance
Is moving at a thousand miles an hour
As the earth is spinning on its axis

And today the sky is solidly white
And all the trees are coated with fresh snow
And the air is interspersed with large flakes
Swirling separately and slowly down

And I realize on this chilly day
In January when the morning is
Marvelous that the sun is resplendent
As it's moving overhead and all that

I am seeing is a reflection of
The penetrating and life-giving light.

Have you not noticed
that this place where
we are living is
exceedingly odd?

It's problematic being me in the
Cold walking outside to and from my car
While managing keys and holding the two
Thermoses of coffee that I need to

Be human and on occasion the load
Is increased with a bag of gym clothes and
A briefcase with the thermoses fitting
Under the crook of an elbow with the

Handles of the bag looping through an arm
But while wearing mittens my fingers are
Mostly useless and then locking my door
And lifting the door of the garage is

An ordeal but I suppose that's just what
Happens when living in Minnesota.

I could always make
two trips back and
forth but that's too
much work.

A girl informed me of Saturday night
Contra dancing where I could always find
A partner and at the same time sashay
And promenade and do a cute little

Turn that is called the do si do with a
Succession of various women of
Different comportment and sizes and
Ages which I enjoy very much and

I would like to go back every week but
When summoned to — swing your girl — I got so
Dizzy and stayed dizzy with visions of
A surging ocean of women whirling

About me that I became light-headed
And had to sit down to regain balance.

I haven't felt so
dizzy since I was
a high school student
chewing tobacco for
the first time.

The oval I am making of my palms
And of my fingers as they are lying
In my lap as my arms are relaxing on
My thighs as I am expressing the

Lotus position and meditating
Before leaving home — the oval of my
Hands are gently focusing my thoughts as
They are arising and passing as I

Am weighing the emotion tinged with every
Thought and discovering whether I am
Adverse attracted or neutral about
A thought and the most helpful part of my

Practice is not to cling to any thought
But learning to let go of every thought.

The uncluttered mind
is like a ball bouncing
down a mountain
stream
unhindered.

I wonder whether it's tiresome to
Read so many of my poems about
Sunrises while noticing my neglect
Of sunsets which are equally lovely

But sunrises are an inspiration
To me while a setting sun is weirdly
Disorienting and disquieting
As the light is vanishing revealing

The preponderance of a void sprinkled
About with pinpoints of starlight teasing
Me with questions and yearnings I have no
Way of satisfying — the questions are

A visceral trembling of spirit
And the yearning is for reassurance.

I just believe there
is something about the
balancing of day and
night hinting of the
imperishable.

When I am quiet enough there is the
Reverberation of my heart and the
Pulsation of my blood in my veins to
Accompany me and for the moment I

Don't have to think about the series of
Chores that weighs on my mind today and the
Challenge of performing a task and of
Satisfying the expectations of

My colleagues and of myself and for
The moment there is the simple pleasure
Of being apart from achievement and
Disappointment and then I recognize

There is a sanctuary within me
Apart from the clamor of my doings.

And then the sustenance
of mind and body
takes over and I move
doing
business.

He has never accepted his brushing
Like the others keeping aloof at a
Distance watching and knowing when I was
Through with them that I would come and stretch him

Before me facing him away from me
As I stroked him with the Furminator
Which is a sturdy brush with metal teeth
As every so often he'd turn and hiss

At me asserting his denial of
My diminution of his dominance
But over the years he's gotten playful
Turning on his back and grasping at the

Brush with his paws and kicking with his back
Legs and sometimes taking the brush from me.

Kitcat manages the brush
as best he can holding
the brush with his paws
moving his face over
the metal teeth.

He flips over exposing his furry
Belly knowing my irresistible
Urge compelling me with my fingertips
To touch his softness while he's alert his

Mouth is open ready to bite his eyes
Are excited expectant and I can't
Resist and grasp his face with a hand while
He swivels about with his spine kicking

With the nails of his back legs biting my
Hand as I'm spinning him about using
Both hands grabbing and slapping so quickly
He can't respond and seems a little stunned

Swiping with his — nail-less — front paws at my
Hands but more often than not he misses.

Grabbing and lifting slightly
Kitcat's haunches while he's
on his back excited
I seize control as he can't
bite swipe or kick.

Johnnie used to be more affectionate
But now he's skinny and thinking mostly
About eating yowling at me when I
Enter the home following me around

Even though he eats more than Kitcat does
Kitcat being twice the size of Johnnie
With Kitcat pouncing continuously
On Johnnie leaving tufts of hair on the

Floor though when I'm present I'll shoo Kitcat
Force Kitcat to release his grip stop him
From biting Johnnie about the neck make
Kitcat slink away while later I see

Both of them curling sleeping together
On a chair in blessed unconsciousness.

Old
skinny
hungry
bullied —
I'd sleep too
if I were Johnnie.

When I'm awake in the hours before dawn
I dwell on the hairline cracks that emerged
Within my family over the years
In a household empty of my children

And a spouse when I would much rather be
Sleeping but somehow I'm not managing
To turn my mind off — I've cleaned out the
Refrigerator but haven't gone through

The cupboards or decided which of the
Pots pans spices and utensils to keep
As dozens of items bespeak the love
My wife displayed in making our dinners —

There is the pot we used to brew our tea
And the knives that cut the chicken and fish.

Somehow our love
wasn't sufficient to
keep the family from
fracturing and wondering
why is painful.

Enso

Zen calligraphers make a circular
Motion with a brush creating in a
Swirl of ink and horsehair a symbol for
The way energy is manifesting

In the eddies of whirlpools and typhoons
In the cycling of daylight and night
In the repetition of the seasons
In the orbits of stars and galaxies

And even in the irresistible
Transitions from birth and exuberant
Youth to the maturation of middle
Age into the sober decline of death —

It's easier for me to believe death
Is a season in the cycles of life.

A crest of sunlight
is continuously
breaking upon the
earth revolving
about its axis.

I notice when a chickadee appears
In the bush beyond my window and it
Is hopping and darting its head about
Then suddenly it flits away — sometimes

I see a group of crows stabbing and
Tearing the carcass of a squirrel on
On the street — and they accommodate my
Passing car by flying away — I am

Aware of the persisting cold when snow
Is covering the ground and the roots of
The trees are embedded in frozen soil
In February and when seeing the

Bare branches and a blue sky I wonder
What would the gnawing of hunger be like?

Do the crows and
chickadees notice
a glorious open sky
while starving in
winter?

I'm looking for a woman with whom I
Could behave just like I do with Kitcat
When seeing Kitcat dozing in a chair
As I'm hoisting him in the air using

His shoulders as a grip gazing into
His eyes suspending his limpness turning
Him left and right hugging him to my chest
Getting his hair all over my shirt and

When returning Kitcat to his chair I
Pet him repetitiously rubbing him
One hand after another from his head
To his tail applying quite vigorous

Pressure and I know Kitcat enjoys it
Because he follows me asking for more.

Such exuberance
on a first date
is liable to
encounter
resistance.

I gained traction in my life after years
Of aimless effort by creating a
Sanctuary in the morning letting
My thoughts percolate listening to words

I heard yesterday attending to the
Emotion conveyed recognizing my
Grief and disappointment wallowing in
Sadness being critical and watching

Criticism dissipate considering
What to do repeating nonsense phrases
Enunciating ridiculous noise
Entertaining my cats shaving my face

Opening the curtains of the windows
Anticipating the sunlight later.

Problems need addressing
emotions are expressed
energy emerges
enthusiasm comes —
I don't know how.

I don't do anything without purpose
Even though I admit I often have
Nonsensical rationales like watching
Many murder investigations for

Self-improvement and the *dharma* says that
Sitting in meditation should be done
Apart from the lure of benefit — that
The epitome of refinement is —

Purposelessness — but really I must say
I practice Zen in the morning because
It quiets my thinking and provides my
Kinder and optimistic impulses

The liberation they need to blossom
Which generates such enthusiasm.

My joyful
nonsensical
exclamations
to my cats have
no purpose.

Every Saturday night there are dances
At the Tapestry Center where I can
Go instead of being alone and they
Know each other very well but also

Welcome newcomers and yes the moment
Came when lining up without a partner
When people looked away and I felt a
Pang but then a gentleman smiled and gave

Place when the fiddling began and we
Were swinging and exchanging partners some
With practiced skill and others not so much
Including me but the rhythmic touching

Holding smiling playing light-heartedly
Was worth the drive to Minneapolis.

Getting used to swinging
and consequent
dizziness is my goal.

So much effort is necessary to
Become a fiddler or a dancer
With a seed of desire serving as
Impetus to blossom into a dance

And I'd like to meet someone to talk with
Joining a light-hearted circle of friends
Indulging in such effervescent joy
Leaving behind a weight of memory

Eliminating apprehension in
A spontaneous celebration of
A kindly graceful motion of people
With the single men and women having

An opportunity to sample each
Other with a swing — could she be the one?

Maybe with
sufficient
swinging
practice
dizziness
goes away?

Apart from the company I had the
Most salient ingredient of the
Afternoon was the brilliantly blue sky
Reflecting off of the fresh fallen snow

With two wisps of clouds on the horizon
And the cold that made the rims of my ears
Much redder as the time passed as Hattie
Informed me in the course of our easy

Conversation as light as wispy clouds
Drifting in an open sky while she was
Pleased with the added stability
That a walking stick provided as we

Meandered on a trail in the prairie
Grassland of the Lake Elmo Park Reserve.

Her poodle Aries kept
putting a ball he was
gripping in his teeth in-
to my hand challenging
me to a tug of war.

I am better off than most of my age
Because I exercise and refrain from
Eating processed foods preferring apples
To potato chips so I'm flexible

And thin about my middle but the growth
Continues persistently regardless
Of my inattention as it's easy
To forget that underneath my socks my

Toenails do need trimming and it is hard
To be pompous scrunching over to the
Left and right twisting a toe getting an
Angle maneuvering the clipper for

A cut and managing my little toes
I can't be thinking about dignity.

I have a
crescendo
of difficulty
scrunching with
my left hand
trimming my left
little toe.

I am a curious mixture of waves
And particles responding with my eyes
And skin to the brilliant light of the sun
With instantaneous electrical

Impulses inside of my brain bringing
To life the drifts of snow outside of my
Window on a day of below zero
Cold that's hard to distinguish from any

Other morning when the sky is open
As the same pinpoint jewels of refracted
Light are visible in the resplendent
Banks of snow but on this morning birds are

Darting strenuously about doing
Whatever they can to keep from freezing.

Waves and particles
come to life and the spare
muscles bones and feathers
of birds endure the
cold and hunger.

My Dad managed sharp edged opinions for
Most of his life that he moderated
By playing Mozart or Shubert for an
Hour in the afternoon every day

On a grand piano and I could tell
Whatever fractious divisions were in
His mind were dissipated in a play
Of ethereal harmony and he

Did his best to pass on his essential
Love to my daughter through lessons and with
The gift of a studio piano
That's residing in my house because she

Hasn't a permanent home and perhaps
Music isn't her love of expression.

The piano is a
symbol of my
Dad's all
encompassing
enthusiasm.

The tiniest twig at the top of a
Cottonwood positions several leaves to
Catch waves of sunlight in summer and the
Whole tree absorbs a prodigious amount

Of radiation with wind stirring leaves
And light sparkling in leaves but in winter
Its branches and craggy bark are exposed
And for a moment the rising sun will

Paint the cottonwood a gorgeous orange
And then the shine fades the light diffuses
And it's revealed as a monstrosity
Of crooks and curves and twists and tangles as

An expression of nature without an
Inch of symmetrical beauty.

But clambering squirrels
and craggy cottonwood
bark are in harmony.

The lines of my property consist of
Right angles and my home is constructed
Of rectangles and triangles but when
I gaze about I see the apple trees

By my driveway with one producing red
The other yellow apples in fall and
Like the cottonwood on the corner by
The street their bare branches are a riot

Of directions apart from notions of
Symmetry surpassing any form of
Predicable pattern presenting me
With a vision of a voracious and

A savage appetite for sunlight that
With the tepid winter sun is absent.

The sight and scent
of apple blossoms
enticing the bees
is a bold display
of seduction.

I do believe that death is only a
Season of life and that a consciousness
Continues apart from memory and
Habit with minutest particles and

Distant galaxies playing their parts to
Spring into being this moment after
Another falling of snow leaving this
Morning the pinpoint sparkles of light in

The fresh snow that seeing somehow brings such
Peace and nourishment to me however
I'll be emoting later whatever
I'm able to believe with limited

Comprehension somehow something says to
Me there is no need to struggle so much.

The tiniest flakes
are falling straight
down here and there
and too tiny to be
snow.

Wisps of diffuse clouds are drifting at a
Lackadaisical pace this morning as
I am marveling at their feathery
Existence floating eastwards in a sky

Of a soothing shade of blue savoring
Their ethereal forms entertaining
Notions of destiny questioning
Whether it is really possible that

These clouds mingling with the sun and wind
Could ever become so smothering and
Weighty that they would have to disperse
And descend in the form of snow or rain

To become inexorably absorbed
In a current moving to the ocean.

Earth
air
fire
water
questions.

Sometimes a surprising inspiration
Comes to me giving me a gift of a
Glimpse of insight into the way things are
And I often smile with recognition

As an unarticulated hunch in
The form of a vaguely comprehended
And nagging but unaddressed conundrum
That was percolating underneath the

Conscious level of my awareness has
Finally resolved itself into a
Burst of clarity while I am walking
From one room and into another and

I will laugh with the joy of solving a
Dilemma I didn't know that I had.

Sometimes
on arriving at the
window I discover
that the inspiration
is forgotten.

Before we extended our knowledge we
Could endow the heavenly bodies with
Spirit and what a mystique the waxing
And waning moon would hold appearing so

Huge and orange on the horizon and
So distant and silver among the stars
While sometimes penetrating the morning
Or the afternoon beyond the clouds as

If to say remember the light of day
Is temporary and wouldn't we have
Savored the mystery of not knowing
How far away and how large it was but

Now we aim our radar at the moon and
Bounce our beams of careful calculation.

We know the earth is
a jewel of the cosmos
because we savor photos
of the earth taken
from the moon.

On occasion I doubt myself second
Guessing the quality of the choices
I make for instance when in connection
With other poets I notice they will

Compose a title for every poem
Providing a table of contents for
Easy reference and I have compared
My paucity of titles as a fault

But today I realized from day to
Day from quatrain to quatrain indeed there
Are breaks within the flow but really the
One hundred poems composing a book

For me signify the modulations
Of one joyously alive harmony.

So pick a page
any page and
see if something
communicates to you
of essential liveliness.

After he's partaken of the canned food
And also of the dry food that comes from
A bag Kitcat will jump onto the shelves
To a space that's next to a microwave

And he proceeds to caterwaul in his high
Pitched voice and he stares at me and will not
Be quiet which is how he behaves when
He wants to be fed which is a nuisance

Trick that he learned from Johnnie so I ask —
What do you want — and he looks me in the
Eyes because he's achieved a stature
Of height at eye level with me which is

Why I think he makes the effort to jump
There and insistently he inquires.

I use my fingertips
massaging the hair
between his ears and
inside his ears and he
shakes his head.

Upon arriving at my place of work
Which is the home where my mom is living
I enter through the garage and into
The printing room and see the printing press

That is a Ryobi press capable
Of printing 11 by 17
Or 8 ½ by 11 inch
Paper which are sizes my Dad and I

Used to print the journal that we published
Which I continue to publish after
Dad died and the Ryobi was rendered
Obsolete by the emergence of much

Better copiers so everyday I'm
Reminded of how the past is fleeting.

A running printing
press has a mechanical
and satisfying
rhythm that I
am missing.

I've concluded there comes a point within
Winter when exhaustion is established
After which the days become a dreary
Trudge to the horizon and I suggest

That February is a state of mind
Not necessarily corresponding
To the calendar as I have known a
Series of blizzards in March even in

April bearing down upon me as one
Continuous never-ending nadir
With no better name than February
Even as the shadowy wings of night

Are diminishing the light of day is
Strengthening if only in mockery.

Yet the sun shines in
February and at
the nadir the only
direction is better
eventually.

**Dedicated to Mike Finley
King of the St. Paul Poets**

We know the thousands and thousands of stars
Glimmering in the vast emptiness of
The night are accompanied by trillions
And trillions of stars that human eyes are

Incapable of seeing — we know that
Each photon of light lingers within a
Gaseous sphere for thousands and thousands of
Years before it discharges into space —

We know that the velocity of light
Is unsurpassable — and we know that
The pinprick points of light surrounding the
Earth have traveled billions and billions of

Years to penetrate a moment of our
Waking consciousness amidst our slumbers.

And yet each human
breath following breath
evinces a continuing
and precious
liveliness.

When I find myself awake a couple
Of hours before dawn with my thoughts cycling
Uselessly I have a choice to lie in
Bed exhausted or to put my cushions

Out and meditate so last night I sat
Determined to quell the cogitation
While Kitcat pounded on the door forcing
Me to rise and let him enter because

He wouldn't stop while Johnnie came to whine
At me because that is what he does while
Kitcat jumped from the bed scampering as
Fast as he could bolting out of the room

So I tossed Johnnie out and closed the door
When Kitcat pounced on him and Johnnie yowled.

Before dawn my
cats are watching
and waiting for
me to move.

Inside of a room cluttered with things that
Supported a printing process that is
Not ongoing — like a light table in the
Corner for laying out copy — I come

Everyday with a sense of gratitude
Because this room inside a house on the
Earth rolling on its axis around
The solar system and the Milky Way

Is here for me when the freshest light of
The ascending sun is entering through
The window and brightening the debris
Of life while I am sitting at my desk

Seizing morning clarity distilling
Experience and cavorting with words.

I have meandered
over several continents
consuming decades
unfocused dissatisfied
finally finding joy.

Breath continues breath blossoming inside
Of lungs and dispersing as a tonic
Throughout my body and inspiring
Me with clarity of mind once I've learned

The trick of attending to the lively
Process of breathing inhaling through my
Nose and releasing as a glorious
Relaxation peacefully quietly

Appreciating the sun and earth and
Leaves and oxygen and nitrogen and
Atmosphere even with the bare branches
Of February breath continues breath

And I don't have to focus attention
Or lift a finger to make it happen.

The simplicity
of breathing
is a gift.

On the verge of March
a thaw is biting drifts of
snow and water is
flowing across the streets down
to the current under ice.

— *Tekkan*

Everyday Mind XIV

A couple of clouds
drifting southeast
give the morning
a gentle air
of evanescence.

It's joyous to have a year every four
Years that we are calling leap year within
Which there is an extra day inserted
In the calendar on February

29 because people are surprised
And befuddled and if you read as I
Do a daily meditation book you
Discover February 29

Isn't there which is like being given
A gift of day on which the demands
Of time are extinguished and the aging
Process is dissolved so I exult as

If I were a bored and overburdened
Student presented with a holiday.

Our best technology
can't keep pace with
the earth's elliptical
orbit around the
sun.

I groaned with the realization of
An unavoidable dilemma
Impacting so powerfully because
Of my habitual inattention

To detail as I recognized I can't
Take part in the poetry instruction
Offered by Donna who intrigues me and
Also attend the annual meeting

Of my Zen Bridge group at exactly the
Same time and what do I do wanting to
Admire Donna and know her better
While also looking forward to being

With so many of my optimistic
Friends celebrating our togetherness?

I can only put off
deciding for another
day as Saturday is
coming.

My daughter came to request some things from
The house for my ex-wife and she asked for
The family photos making me question
What to do and I decided to let

Them go even as I knew that they are
Poignant memories that can't be relived
With me remembering differently from
Her and from my daughter and my son as

I can only see them with the lens of
Today as if my present view were of
Conclusions and consequences with a
Weight of emotions as no one else could

Look at them and have the feelings that we
Do even as our feelings will differ.

Seeing the family photos
ten years from now
how much and
what would I
remember?

Jason said that Jupiter's massive presence
Orbiting the sun as it does further
From the sun than the earth is serving as
A shield deflecting or absorbing the

Cosmic debris that otherwise would strike
The earth and then Jason talked about a
Phenomenon called the Barycenter
That determines the point around which the

Planets orbit the sun that is not at
The center of the sun but rather at
A point that is the central pivot of
Mass in motion that sounds so overly

Complicated to me as scientists
Answer the questions that I didn't ask.

The way things are
gets increasingly
complex for clever
people who keep on
asking questions.

I look at the moon seeing it change its
Shape and position high and low in the
Night and I believe before people were
Living in cities and filling the night

With fluorescence and neon and before
Our busy days were consumed with details
As we are now checking our calendars
And staring at our cell phones in our hands

Before electronics hypnotized us
I believe the mystical allure of
The moon must have been so much more potent
So much more of a stimulant for the

Peoples of the earth to ponder visions
Of heaven searching for reassurance.

How much more of a
jewel of the night and
the morning and
the afternoon the moon
must have been.

Apart from our reading communities
Where we share our enthusiasm in
Small gypsy-like gatherings and apart
From the marketing strategy and the

Tech savvy endeavor of composing
Books and the eyes-straining hunt for typos
For correction of inarticulate
Grammar or word choice and the swings from pride

To self-loathing that come with managing
Large numbers of my poems I love the
Sanctuary of pushing distractions
Aside for an hour of clarity

In the morning when I can play with words
And discover what in me needs getting out.

The simplest details have
enormous consequence —
once free of distraction
joy emerges.

Half my life is spent within the darkness
Of night without my thinking about it
But I know that there are trillions of stars
Beyond the few that I can see and I

Know that gravity is crushing inward
That nuclear fusion is exploding
Outwards of every star in a balance
Of nature persisting for billions of

Years and that the velocity of light
Proceeding from a star extending in
All directions is the speediest force
Of nature and yet the light takes billions

Of years from distant stars to reach the earth
And perhaps those stars no longer exist.

There are trillions
and trillions of
stars and yet
darkness
predominates.

The words and lines of my sonnets make a
Straight edge along the left margin while the
Right side is unpredictable because
Even though every line will consist of

Ten syllables the syllables vary
In length which leads me to reflect on how
Regimented effort with guidelines goes
Well with the happy exploration of

Possibility inescapably
Relying upon the conventional
Meaning of words and the habitual
Idioms of the culture I want to

Discover whether I can say something
Worthy of seizing a reader's interest.

An empty sky with
only the daylight passing
through upon the earth
is a transitory and
glorious experience.

My everyday mind consists of little
Insights hardly worthy of notice that
I wouldn't be attending to at
All except for my meditation that's

Revealing to me that naturally
My thoughts are like a ball bouncing down a
Mountain stream unhindered by obstacles
Until emotions get entangled with

Situations making scenarios
Causing me to experience the self-
Created dissatisfaction easy
To fall into and so difficult to

Escape until I recall my thoughts are
Like a ball bouncing down a mountain stream.

Naturally thoughts may
be unhindered by
obstacles if I allow
them to come
and go.

Fear of being rejected was hard to
Overcome but on Match.com I read
Hundreds of profiles gazed at photos
Ventured a formula greeting became

Indifferent to the non-responses
Developing persistence opening
Possibilities returning more than
Once meeting women listening learning

Conversing sampling differences
Transcending my inhibitions playing
With words dreaming anticipating
While needing to reschedule appointments

Cindy on Tuesday Ruth on Thursday and
Lori Friday Cookie this afternoon.

Enticing with
poetry
Xia
Keesa
Joan.

Every poem embodies the seeds of
Poems to be written just as every
Day contains the seeds of approaching days
As my attention is naturally

Drawn to the permutations of the sky
As what a revelation comes when a
Sky with daylight drains away to the west
Presenting such looming questions about

The odd experience of living on
A rotating earth orbiting a sun and
Possessing dormant and growing seasons
As today is overcast and chilly

While yesterday was sunny and warmer
Perfect for our walking around the lake.

Walking around Lake
Harriet with Cookie
I discovered a
beautiful woman I'd
like to know better.

Thank you for talking with me today as
We had the time for expressing ourselves
With me talking about my conundrums
Being enthusiastically a poet

A sober alcoholic a Buddhist
And a conservative politically
With each group of my association
Misapprehending every other group

Which complicates how freely I'm able
To express myself even as I try to
Be transparent and welcoming it's the
Political animosity that's

Currently separating everyone
Into groups despising other groups.

Communication
is easiest with
sober alcoholics
and with my
two cats.

I sometimes wonder what would it be like
To go to sleep and never wake up but
In the everyday world I've come to look
For the little changes signaling the

Shifting into another season as
There was a dusting of snow overnight
In the midst of much warmer days with the
Melting of three months of snow from the ground

While the frost is leaving the earth as I
Noticed this morning it's comfy now to
Walk about the floorboards of my home in
Bare feet again but in Minnesota

We are not so easily fooled into
Believing that spring is almost arrived.

The dusting of snow
reminds me a thaw
in March is often
followed by blizzards
in April.

We are particles and waves coming to
Being with chemicals and molecules
Each of us with beating hearts and breathing
Lungs that beat and breathe of themselves without

Any effort of conscious awareness
Just as the sun combusts itself with a
Balance of gravity crushing inward
Nuclear fusion exploding outwards

Radiating life giving energy
And in my isolation I may think
There's so much exertion necessary
There are so many details to control

I can't possibly succeed of myself
Without taking responsibility.

Being responsible
or letting go
is an exquisitely
balanced pivot
point.

There weren't tests available when I was
Feeling lightheaded and I disbelieved
The power of the Coronavirus
And I ventured to the gym lifted the

Heaviest weights and pedaled on the bike
Vigorously for an hour keeping
My distance from people ignoring the
Virus putting faith in my attitude

When breathing became much more difficult
And not moving necessary as the
Asthma of my body can't be denied
No matter how athletic I am so

I became a spectator lying on
My back watching the broadcasting of news.

Minnesota Governor
Walz ordered the
gyms in the state
closed for at least
two weeks.

I am circulating air about
Myself by inhaling and exhaling
Exactly as the people in China
Did where the pandemic virus arose

A month ago while Saturday night was
A tipping point when I discovered it's
Easiest to breathe when lying flat on
My back and not moving while remaining

Calm perusing a series of murder
Investigations on a cable channel
Occupying me semi-consciously
As turning to my side would congest my

Lungs but being perfectly still seemed to
Open the way to continuous breath.

Calm and rest
in the midst of
difficult breathing
opens a narrow
way to tomorrow.

In every nation businesses and schools
Are closing and people are avoiding
Each other being afraid of catching
The virus through our breathing or handling

Tainted items as the news is broadcast
Continuously with the government
Organizing health care infrastructure
Broadcasting assurance and instructions

Projecting an aura of confidence and
Calm urging everyone to minimize
Contact with each other and to shelter
At home until the wave of infection

Has done its worst while our livelihoods are
Interrupted into difficult months.

Infection
ripples into
chaos.

Society is upside down today
With some people working and others not
As the federal and state governments
Are preventing the gatherings of large

Groups of people and are discouraging
The meeting of more than ten people so
Schools and businesses are closed for at least
Two weeks depending on how successful

The containment of the virus will be
But our enforced separation from each
Other reveals how much I'm depending
On you as you're depending on someone

Who's depending on others as each of
Us is connected to everyone else.

We are
tethered
by breath
words
intentions
decisions
behavior.

Television is gluing everyone
Together with announcements informing
The public of the stay-at-home orders
And of the money to be sent from the

National treasury to each needy
American and of the production
Of anti-virus medications while
I am playing with my phone and using

My fingertips and reading articles
Logging in for videoconferences
With friends in sobriety and I am
Whimsically exploring for love by

Holding the phone lightly to my ear and
Listening to the voices of women.

Voices inside my
head expand
horizons lighten
gloom soothing
isolation.

A blustery wind is swaying the bare
Branches as lines of geese are laboring
To stay in formation high amidst the
Yet higher swirling of clouds within which

The sun is making an occasional
Appearance as on the ground the streets are
Empty with only a jogger or a
Person walking a dog ambling along

As people are adhering to advice
Are not mingling in restaurants or cafes
Not doing unnecessary commerce
Are shut in their homes until the proper

Officials determine the spread of the
Virus has been contained and we can breathe.

Fortunate people
can work from home
while others are
without jobs for
who knows how long?

My home is full of a lot of junk from
Twenty years of raising a family
With the kids grown and gone with the ex-wife
Taking her things when she can so I'm left

With toys video games and books and clothes
With the furniture I want rid of with
Closets and drawers full of people's stuff
That I haven't looked at or touched for years

And all of it has been collecting dust
Interspersed with repairs I've neglected
Because I've been busy with exercise
With operating my publication

But now the gym is closed and I'm out of
Excuses for not redoing my home.

The things in my house
gradually amidst the
discord of my family
became an unbearable
weight upon my mind.

March is dripping every minute with the
Snow on the ground slowly disappearing
Into the sodden grass and soil as mist
Is lingering between the trees and homes

While it's difficult to distinguish the
Sky from the mist with the bare branches so
Jumbled wildly and weirdly still within
The absence of a wind or a bird as

The twisting and turning of the branches
And twigs slowly emerging in the gray
Morning light bespeak an aggressive and
Explosive energy latent at the

Moment within the overhanging and
Dominating quiescence of the trees.

Turning
twisting
bare
twigs
portend an
appetite
for sunlight.

The gyms in Minnesota are closed to
Prevent the spreading of the virus which
Imposes a hole in my routine so
For exercise I run up and down the

Stone steps at the southern end of downtown
Stillwater to the top of a limestone
Bluff attracting the fitness freaks from miles
Away whom I encounter and compare

Myself against on my first day running
Briskly ascending descending five times
Achieving satisfaction until the
Morning afterwards when walking was quite

Excruciating reminding me its
Easy to start and hard to keep going.

I try to count the steps
while ascending
but get confused
coming up with
different sums.

Radio television Internet
Communicate the decisions of the
Politicians and medical experts
Determined to impede the virus by

Halting all but essential commerce for
No one knows how long as we are advised
To keep distance between us because we
Don't want to be Italy overwhelmed

With too many patients struggling for
Breath and not enough ventilators to
Rescue everyone as America
Is manufacturing ventilators

Preparing vaccines experimenting
With available and effective drugs.

Doctors and nurses
are exposed
overwhelmed
without equipment
and masks.

Cable airwaves are transmitting sniping
Criticism over the president's
Braggadocio and unwarranted
Optimism as commentators are

Touting opinion polls while arguing
With each other and attempting to be
Cogent but there's only so much noise on
TV that's bearable while this morning

I noticed the birds have resumed singing
Almost all the snow is gone the soil is
Moist the grass though mostly pale is exposed
To an increasingly strengthening sun

And the presence of the trees inspires
An anticipation of budding leaves.

Soon breezes will be
sounding in the leaves
again while I can
awaken to birdsong
through open windows.

The margin on the left of this poem
Is aesthetically pleasing to my eye
Upholding the effusive expression
Of words as words are skipping across the

Page as the margin is a boundary
Serving an organizing principle
Creating for a series of poems
One upon another the spine of a

Book while the words are an attempt to seize
And embody an ephemera of
Insight and emotion hopefully in
A form communicating a zestful

Experience between a writer and
A reader dissolving separation.

An open book
relies upon a spine
as a glue cohering
something of our fleeting
experience together.

Walking up the steep incline of Myrtle
Street I noticed on my north the roughly
Hewn blocks of limestone characteristic
Of Stillwater stacked upon each other

Forming a wall holding the persisting
Pressure of a hill of earth day after
Day perhaps from the decades when the town
Was a frontier refuge for lumberjacks

Taking a holiday from harvesting
White pine and because the size of each block
Is formidably heavy the massive
Undertaking of construction without

Consideration of delicacy
Makes me think of the brawny lumberjacks.

They were savvy
engineers of force sizing
up the necessary weight
of stone blocks balancing
the assertion of the earth.

The prosaic limestone wall on Myrtle
Street is a world away from the lofty
Inca palace of Machu Picchu set
Upon a tropical pinnacle of

The Andes mountains created more than
Six hundred years ago so precisely
Fitting the much more massive blocks of stone
Without mortar and astronomically

Aligned designed not to hold back the earth
But to express a harmony amidst
The clouds and stars with ancient techniques we
Cannot comprehend today but in praise

We can designate the temple of the
Sun and the chamber the three windows.

Stillwater witnessed
the frontier passage of
burgeoning industry —
Machu Picchu evinces
vanished aristocracy.

Everything is flawed from a painful point
Of view whether the trouble is cancer
Financial difficulty persisting
Loneliness bearing the injustice of

False accusation being the target
Of political persecution or
Having the prosaic habit of a
Negative attitude and even if

A person is safe and unaffected
While others are miserable the tinge
Of apprehension is palpable and
I wish life were otherwise but if it's

Any consolation we don't suffer
Alone and get through trouble together.

The self-absorption
of suffering comes and
goes in relation to the
presence of love.

The president extended the guideline
Another thirty days until the end
Of April advising nonessential
Workers to stay-at-home to limit the

Spread of infection as hotels and parks
And stadiums are converted into
Hospitals as General Motors and
Ford are making ventilators as a

Speedy test for the virus is coming
With the estimate of peak infection
In two weeks with 100,000 to
200,000 fatalities while

Politicians bicker thus becoming
A menace to America's morale.

Wash hands often
clean household surfaces
avoid touching the face
about the mouth nose and eyes
interdicting the virus.

We talked about whether aspen trees were
Conscious of people walking in their midst
When Jason remarked as he and I were
Walking in William O'Brien State Park

That aspen trees aren't like other trees as
They aren't separate from each other but
They come from a shared system of roots and
They are all a single organism

And yes perhaps they emanate a kind
Of consciousness different from ours and
Because Jason is an ecologist
Who understands the evolution and

Interconnection of landscape plants and
Animals his words are penetrating.

Ten thousand years ago
this land was covered
by a sheet of ice without
vegetation or habitation
possible.

We were walking amidst a lower stretch
Of a trail that used to be the course of
The St. Croix River with the spring melting
Of snow and the pooling of water when

The air was full with the overlapping
Ticking of chorus frogs that sounded like
Cicadas to me with the chuckling calls
Of wood frogs and with the peep peep peeping

Of a few of the spring peeper frogs as
Jason predicted that they would become
Quiet as we passed by while the frogs were
Invisible to me when suddenly

The air was empty of sound but alive
With intelligent anticipation.

Jason thrives exploring
the fabric of consciousness
discounting the supposed
superiority of
people.

The queen conch is long gone leaving only
A shell behind that I retrieved from the
Recesses of my basement giving it
A dusting revealing the charm of its

Curving inward lip so brightly pink and
Its curving outward lip so glossy white
Which inspired me to do what people
Are supposed to do which is to hold the

Hollowness of the conch seashell to my
Ear to supposedly hear an echo
Of the reverberating ocean and
Maybe I heard the faintest whispering

Maybe I was only imagining
As I was listening attentively.

Maybe the cosmos
was listening to me
in the form of a
queen conch seashell that
resembles an ear.

Fifth Avenue is empty of people
Which is strange for New York City as the
Army Corps of Engineers is making
Field Hospitals in Central Park and in

The Javits Center as the city is
Acquisitioning beds from the vacant
Hotels while the nurses and doctors are
Overworked and are catching the virus

No different from doctors and nurses
In Michigan Illinois Florida
And Louisiana while in the rest
Of America the people aren't so

Oppressed though everyone is staying
Home and keeping distance from each other.

Consuming news
Americans risk
infection from
petty reporters
and politicians.

Thinking is so easy to do without
The slightest effort and I don't want to
Stop my cogitation because it's quite
Amusing when I'm balanced and besides

Without a storehouse of thoughts how could I
Converse with friends which is a pleasure I
Couldn't live without but I practice Zen
To let my thoughts come and go by holding

Them gently within the oval I am
Making of my hands sampling in the
Process the tang of emotion attached
To every thought practicing the skill of

Letting go of thought feeling as I do
The dissolution of disturbances.

What my mind does
to weigh me down with
entanglements is a
habit I don't have to
entertain.

I gave my ex-wife all of our photos
Without hesitation but while going
Through the debris of her room looking in
In a box I discovered photos of

A Christmas more than twenty years ago
Of brightly wrapped presents under a tree
Of kittens long since grown and passed away
Of my wife and me without wrinkles and

She is so beautiful and I am young
Again but what's stunning are the happy
Faces of our children Joshua and
Jocelyn innocent and joyous

Before they went to elementary
School and our home was a sanctuary.

The faces of our children
without a hint of
apprehension are
bursting with love.

We are connected electronically
Seeing each other's faces on-line having
Video streaming conferences taking
The communication we need during

Our physical distancing while we are
Advised to wear masks when shopping for food
Because in the intensive care units
Of hospitals across America

People with the virus are struggling
Reducing their focus of awareness
Grasping the next breath feeling as if their
Lungs were filled with glass terrifying the

Nurses and doctors who are caring for
Them so vulnerable to infection.

The fulcrum of
America's effort to
contain the virus is
separation.

The bicycle is heavy with large tires
And riders on racing bikes are passing
Me and frustrating me but there is
The afternoon sun and chilly breezes

And the scenery downtown Stillwater
And a lengthy stretch along the river
Leading to an avenue in the sky
Called the Crossing Bridge taking me into

The Wisconsin countryside where I
Turn about for home while throughout my ride
From the spring-time flooding of the river
And from the wayside ponds I'm noticing

Something new to me that Jason revealed
On our walk — the ticking of chorus frogs

The steep incline of
Myrtle Street at the
end of my ride where
I gasp for breath
is on my mind.

A blustery day yanks on the roots of
Trees agitating and spurring them into
A resurrection of the budding leaves
While I am striving on my bicycle

Leaving the shield of an embankment and
Ascending the extended approach to
The Crossing Bridge in the open air and
I am pedaling vigorously and

Buffeted by the wind at a lofty
Height that only the birds experience
Making me resort to a lighter gear
Straining against the ragged surges of

Wind with labored breath and wearied legs I
Admire the feathery aplomb of birds.

The hill and homes
block the northeast wind
as I ascend Myrtle Street
against the gradient.

I haven't got the gist of using the
Video capacity of the app
So I can hear my sober friends but can't
See them for the online meeting and

Today there are new people from distant
Places whom I haven't met so I use
The quality and emphasis of their
Voices to convey personality

Allowing my imagination to
Form an image of their faces but I
Recognize most of us from many years
Of experience and the message is

Always the same — not to drink today — and
I look forward to seeing the new ones.

Grasping sobriety
can be like climbing
a rope hand over hand —
or like giving a friend
a hand up.

Words are always disputable which is
What I discovered when a friend and I
Started a writer's group in Kyoto with
A master poet named Cid Corman and

Cid brought excellent poetry to read
And he challenged every word that I wrote
And because I hadn't digested life
Enough I gave up poetry for Zen

When years later a poem burst from me
Prompting me to ransack everyday mind
To examine every sensation and
To question every fleeting perception

To seek for ways to dispel delusion
And now I need to learn how to relax.

The mind is a bowl
open to the cosmos
once the clamor
of thinking becomes
quiet.

The lake was reflecting the overcast
Sky in ripples characteristic of
Water so fluidly and even though
It was a gray day in spring I could see

Brightness testifying to the power
Of the sun that despite a covering
Of clouds everything was visible with
Razor clarity with geese among the

Reeds across the far side of the water
Their honking reaching us from a distance
As we were talking about having friends
The difficulty of loneliness and

The weight of broken relationships and
Dog food at a hundred dollars a month.

Your life rotates about
walking with Aries
your poodle two or three
times a day.

The gradient of Myrtle Street rises
Precipitously but it's becoming
Less intimating with each ascent
As it rises in two sections with a

Flatter part in-between and the
First section is only a taste of
Happy difficulty to come when I
Settle on the proper gear and rise from

The seat and stand running on the pedals
Seeing the cracks on the street heart beating
Lungs filling exhaling at the limit
Of capacity determination

Wavering with glimpses up to a bend
Around which I finally see the top.

At the top is
victory
satisfaction
just a little
easier this time.

It's been too cold for the bicycle for
Several days because a northern front has
Descended on Minnesota at the
Very tipping point of spring and so for

Sanity in my isolation I
Am walking for exercise watching the
Snow melting upon the pavement for an
Afternoon that is an oddity of

The temperature being much colder
Above and not so much below as I
Am striding over the Crossing Bridge with
The wind battering my body and face

And forcing me to almost close my eyes
Seeing snow falling sideways in the wind.

A warm snow is
lashing me about
and the river below is
invisible.

They appear again in spring about as
Numerous as the squirrels while keeping their
Distance from people though they aren't afraid
To gaze at us for a moment before

Scampering away and seeing their mode
Of ambulation does make me think of
The kangaroo sharing elongated
Hind legs and powerful haunches designed

For springing jumps which in practice gives them
An odd hopping gait and they also have
The kangaroo's lengthy ears and somewhat
Pointy nose but as they're little creatures

It's easy to overlook their presence
Unless a person is a gardener.

I don't care for
growing flowers
or vegetables so I've
got nothing against
the rabbits.

The lampshade in the corner is glowing
Yellow of a tint less brightly and more
Gentle than the light dispersed onto the
Walls below the shade as the sun rising

In the east is now prominent enough
To pour itself into the living room
From the west window to clarify the
Studio piano the drawing of

The Chinese man and the wooden table
As the back of the steel stop sign across
The street is transformed by the angle of
The sun into a brilliant disk of light

Becoming almost another sun as
Painful to look at as the sun itself.

I can see the
sun touching
the branches of
the lilac bush
on the corner

While I was walking over the lofty
St. Croix Crossing Bridge and seeing such a
Panorama of clouds and the mighty
River glimmering in the sunlight so

Far below me I remembered that
William Wordsworth wrote a sonnet about
A quiet morning view of London from
Westminster Bridge as the ships and domes

And theaters and temples of the calm
Majestic city were glistening in the
Silent and smokeless air as described in
His lines arrayed with rhyming ends and I

Took pleasure in imagining the scene
A vanished cynosure of history.

Walking on the Crossing Bridge
I shared something of the
mighty beating heart
that Wordsworth felt
shorn of ornamentation.

A friend whom I would like to know better
Says that I'm more fluent with poetry
Than in our conversation together
Which is an insightful assessment but

I am aware of the tripwires of our
Differences if I disregarded
Would lead to unpleasant disagreements
Making me defensively circumspect

Contrary to my desire as she's not
Aware of how joyfully present I
Could be given a more harmonious
Mixture of personality — which is

No one's fault — so I've fallen into my
Pattern of being a good listener.

Maybe we have to
make do until
the missing pieces
of our puzzles
come together.

At 4:30 a.m. Kitcat rises
On his haunches striking my bedroom door
Like a drum with his front paws one after
The other insisting I get up and

Occasionally I wait testing his
Determination but eventually
I open up and he and Johnnie burst
In with Johnnie whining to be fed while

Kitcat lunges onto the bed and up
On a chest of drawers next to a marble
Urn holding a dozen peacock feathers
And he sniffs licks and nibbles the frilly

Parts every morning trying my patience
When I ask him what he thinks he's doing.

I pick him up
look into his eyes
toss him onto the bed
and he scrambles
away.

I'm hesitant to write about my phone
Because I'm prideful and am mindful that
If someone reads my poem a hundred
Years from now I could be amusing by

Praising the marvelous technology
Allowing me with a hand-held device
To connect to the Internet and with
Satellites thereby accessing so much

Of humanities' collected knowledge
As a person reading a hundred years
From now could be using technology
So superior that he would snicker

At my quaint fascination as if a
Smartphone were like a horse and a buggy.

Do we really expect
technology to keep
quadrupling power
without incurring
nemesis?

People in America for weeks have
Been keeping a distance from each other
To mitigate the spread of the virus
And the actual numbers of the dead

Are far less than the predictions casting
Doubt on the justifications for the
Strangulation of the economy
With the hardship and insecurity

Imposed on those of precarious means
But we will never know how many would
Have died but for the stay-at-home orders
While the burden of providing food and

Care has fallen on doctors nurses truck
Drivers and the supermarket workers.

The cashier
at the local Walmart
processing payments
for groceries is
essential.

A person gets attached to the first cup
Of coffee and to leaving home at a
Normal time to meet a predictable
Group of people even though everything

Is constantly changing with each precious
Friendship destined to disappear some day
It's so easy to be lulled into a
Sense of permanence by a gradual

Pace of metamorphosis making just
A single deviation from the norm
Noticeable when the emergence of
The worldwide pandemic like an earthquake

Upturning the smallest details of life
Moved beyond our grasping the way things were.

But people are
also stubbornly
persistent and
given to mass
amnesia.

Jason takes bounding steps on the trails of
William O'Brien State Park that he walks
For exercise and because he is an
Ecologist he knows why the oaks and the

White paper birch are growing on one side
Of the hill and the juniper are on
The other explaining as he does to
Me as I'm stretching my stride and pace to

Keep the conversation going about
The way sometimes a hunch will bring him to
A stop in the woods almost as if he's
Called by a consciousness of the landscape

Proceeding carefully stepping slowly
To find a lotus that shouldn't be there.

I discover two days
later my left big toenail
is bruised and black because
my socks were too thick
my boots a little too small.

Things happen without my thinking about
Them like the way my eyes are blinking keeping
Themselves moist or the way my tongue is a
Ballerina acrobatically

Flexing and modulating subtle sounds
And I don't have to make a decision
To sneeze or cough as they ambush me with
Vehemence embarrassing me at such

Awkward moments and if I were in charge
Of beating my heart and breathing my lungs
I wouldn't have the pleasure of my quiet
Selections from which my poetry comes

But it is especially marvelous
How a bruised toenail takes care of itself.

An odd pain persisted
from my left big toenail
and now it's blackened
and getting ready to
fall off.

While I am sitting on my cushion and
Meditating the St. Croix Crossing Bridge
Is in my mind along with the clouds the
Sunshine and the buffeting wind that may

Be blowing on me from behind which makes
My pedaling easy or if I'm facing
A crossing or a head wind then my legs
And lungs are stressed because I like to go

As fast as I can as a test of my
Determination as I am sitting
On my cushion meditating as a
Thought flickers and disappears of what I

Want to do this sunny afternoon and
Then I return to pregnant emptiness.

It's hard to specify
what the nourishment
of emptiness is but
I can write about my
bicycle.

A body has to have a harmony
Of parts to compose a sensible form
Of locomotion and it's curious
To say how the creature came to be with

Its tiny front legs and five fingered paws
Opposed to its enormous haunches and
Elongated rear paws balanced by a
Sinewy long tail as a view of the

Whole including lengthy and upright ears
And pointy face seems a concoction of
Absurdity bereft of dignity
Lopsided hopping lopsided hopping

Slowly moving finically about
The earth stooping over to munch the grass.

Only when the
red kangaroo is
springing into speed
is the music of form
revealed.

In the distance the rain was falling in
Barely visible lines of gray but the
Clouds over us were scattered and when we
Stopped to look at them after so many

Hours of vigorous striding and maybe
Because my pulse was elevated and
I was beyond the point of exhaustion
The clouds appeared to be drifting away

So rapidly as if I'd never seen
Them properly before in a moment
Of appreciation that the sky and
Clouds and sun are always overhead as

A counterbalance to entanglements
Providing light and rain and detachment.

Jason and I were
talking about life on
planets and moons
apart from seasons.

We passed copses of aspen interspersed
With white paper birch as Jason would stoop
Over to notice a flowering plant
That wasn't colorful and didn't look

Like a flower to me while he pointed
To the outlines of the glacial river
Ten thousand years ago recounting a
Massive movement of the water leaving

Gravelly sand of coarse and fine grains with
Flat plains at different elevations
Separated by steep slopes and with the
Deposits of sediment in places

Over a hundred feet but not so much
Where bedrock is nearer to the surface.

Beyond the
memorization
of species is every
unique season
with surprising
discoveries.

Most of yesterday was rainy and the
Water soaked into the earth and we have
Had warmer sunny days before yesterday
And have also had rainy days before

Yesterday but we have not yet had a
Soaking rainy day followed by sunny
Warm days surely precipitating the
Voracious upraising growth of the grass

Before yesterday and today we are
Looking forward to a liberating
Spring as every year has a calendar
Demarcation of the end of winter

But a calendar isn't lively and
We know when spring has finally arrived.

All the previously
bare bushes and branches
of trees in the neighborhood
are sprouting bright
little buds.

From year to year the signs of change are hard
To remember whether this far along
In Minnesota it's normal at the
Ending of April for the air to be

So stubbornly chilly in the morning
That the furnace remains useful and the
Windows are better shut as I'm walking
About the house evaluating my

Life in comparison with others when
On stepping out with the trash I see a
Robin perched on a twig of the apple
Tree and hear the robin singing the song

That robins do in the morning and I
Hear the air is alive with singing birds.

Marvelous birds
remind me the very
air is alive with
energy apart from
evaluations.

To a squirrel my cottonwood with its
Enormous width and height would appear as
A pillar upholding the world as it
Towers over everything else and the

Tiniest twigs at the very top would
Mark the furthermost end of a journey
Into space with the deepest grooves of the
Bark serving as a ready highway for

The gripping clambering eagerness of
The squirrel climbing easily around
And around the circular trunk giving
A different and an awesome vista

With every higher turn of the circuit
With each turn a happy exploration.

To a squirrel a
cottonwood is a house
of many mansions
especially when buds
are reappearing.

If I were a squat individual
With a prodigious weight heaped upon me
With four stubby legs situated well
Apart and forming a rectangular

Mode of ambulation limiting my
Forward striding to little steps little
Steps I suppose my attention would be
Focused mostly on the sensations of

The earth and the doings of the soil and
Plants and worms and insects with perhaps an
Occasional tear with a hungry fox
Or a coyote but every itch would be

Unreachable and the sky and the moon
Would be a dimension beyond knowing.

I wonder whether
cognition mirrors
the lassitudinous
gait of the
tortoise?

How small we are in comparison to
Mountains and oceans and deserts and how
Stridently we assert our importance
As the Pyramids of Giza and the

Pillars of Luxor attest as such pains
Were taken to align the places of
Worship and burial with the passage
Of the burning sun over rocks and sand

Yet even with radio telescopes
Detecting evidence of the Big Bang
It seems that we will never escape the
Bounds of our ever-present horizon

In the distance as we are beings quite
Encumbered with an aversion to death.

The earth is round
spinning eastwards
relative to the sun —
the horizon is moving
1000 miles an hour.

In Japan they celebrate the ending
Of April and the beginning of May
As golden week as the penetrating
Cold has departed and the sweltering

Heat has not arrived while cherry trees and
Wisteria are blooming and the air
Is perfectly temperate prompting the
People to gather in the parks spreading

Blankets on the grass under the cherry
Trees for the passing of conversation
While sitting and seeing the precious blue
Light flickering in pink cherry blossoms

As year after year the seasons pivot
With the blooms of cherry evanescence.

On any day
drops of rain
could scatter the
flowering
quickly.

I assumed that the birds were like people
With each bird capable of a medley
Of songs but my walking with Jason is
Dangerous because he exposes my

Misconceptions knowing as he does that
Each type of bird has its own pattern of
Sound recognizable to the others
Of its kind and birders know this because

They've dedicated years to listening
To birds being birds as birders are the
Kind of people who happily do that
Sort of thing noticing the patterns of

Habitation migration markings of
Feathers and the signature mating calls.

Barn swallow — tit-tit-tit-tit
black-crowned night heron — quawlk
black-capped chickadee — fee-bee
black-chinned hummingbird — tchew
blue-gray gnatcatcher — zpeee

In Japan I heard a warbler in spring
Singing from a stand of fir trees and the
Sound was a liquid loveliness that I
Could never have imagined beforehand

And even though the song has passed I do
Remember its effect some thirty years
Ago and I learned that the Japanese
Call the bird the *uguisu* and the

Name is an imitation of its song
The very sound that cast a spell on me
But just reading or reciting the name
Isn't the same as hearing the bird so

Suddenly and unsuspectingly that
Such unearthly beauty is possible.

After the *uguisu*
the walking path became
quiet.

I was aghast when Jason remarked that
The birds are repeating patterns of song
That improvisation isn't their thing
That they aren't like jazz musicians digging

A riff that was a cherished assumption
Of mine because it's disappointing to
Discover without a doubt that I was
Wrong when six books ago I published a

Poem writing emphatically that
The *uguisu* doesn't repeat a
Pattern but because of Jason now I
Know that the *uguisu* in fact does

And I'm grasping for dubious angles
To wriggle out of my exact wording:

Humans listen intently
recreating bird song
into syllables trying
to grasp the ethereal
with a net.

Repetition with variety is
A spice of life as I wonder whether
A robin is capable of singing
Exactly the same song and whether my

Handwriting traces a similar or
A copy of my signature as each
Of my sonnets produces fourteen ten
Syllable lines but sometimes I'm writing

About Jason and other times about
Red Kangaroos — and the earth and moon and
Sun generate predictable patterns
But the timing varies through the years as

Tulips come before cherry and lilac
Blossoms but they are all late this season.

The sky is glorious
red and yellow tulips
are glowing in the
sunrise but it's
as cold as March.

I'm seeing again the leaves coming out
As the tulips are glowing in the light
As little pinkish buds are appearing
On both of my apple trees which I know

From experience will produce lovely
White blossoms with the sweetest scent that I
Have to be close to enjoy which informs
Me that the bumblebees must have better

Noses than I do otherwise why would
The apple tree bother with creating
Perfume so I'm wondering what are the
Lilac bushes doing on the corner

Of my property as I do not see
A hint of their laggardly flowering.

They also produce
the sweetest perfume
with the variety
of three shades
of purple.

With the pandemic continuing we
Sober alcoholics have taken to
Meeting in Pioneer Park sitting well
Apart from each other in the folding

Chairs that each of us brings partaking of
The principles we practice and swapping
Stories with an elevated view of
The valley and the sun-speckled river

Stretching in the distance before us but
What I enjoyed was the brightest spring sky
Scattered with the clouds when I discovered
How lovely it is to lose myself in

The ethereal sight of a single
Cloud drifting and transforming in the wind.

Wisps and wings
curling and stretching
glowing in the light
gray underneath
constantly changing.

I have an idea to assist the
Beleaguered national government in
Our befuddlement and perplexity
Dealing with the Coronavirus and

With the accumulating national
Debt — why don't we mint about a thousand
Trillion dollar coins approximately
The size of Frisbees that could be made of

One hundred percent sterling silver with
The United States Seal on one side and
The image of President Donald Trump
On the other paying for everything

Which could lead to a fascinating game
Of spinning the magic coin through the air.

Whoever caught
a waffling disc
could become an instant
phenomenon —
a *trillionaire*.

After months of seeing the bare branches
They aren't noticeable anymore as
They're just a part of a scenery that
Isn't changing and then the air becomes

Temperate on some days but returns to
Cooler temperatures as the grass is
Green again after rainy days though the
Grass is growing slowly because the air

Remains stubbornly chilly but then on
An afternoon my eyes are opened to
The presence of the leaves again so bright
In the sunshine and everything seems young

Again in the blue light of spring lifting
The glowing clouds transforming in the sky.

Suddenly the leaves
are here swaying
and sighing in the
breezes like friends
returning.

I'm grateful for the gardeners of
Stillwater when I'm driving about town
Because when I'm rushing to do a chore
Their efforts lighten my day with just a

Glance aside on Everett Street to a
Terrace of soil upraising yellow and
Red tulips appearing as splashes of
Happiness that I didn't have to earn

Contemplating as I do the cups of
Tulips radiating the harmony
Of sun and rain and warmth returning for
Another season of growth apart from

Whatever duty is propelling me
I remember there is joy in living.

The tulips are
the sunlight
visible in
exquisite
form.

Round bootlaces were like thorns sticking in
My toes as nothing so dissipates my
Dignity as having to keep bending
Over to retie the damn bootlaces

But then Jason showed me how to double
Knot the laces — go over and under
And then make the rabbit ears and then tie
The rabbit ears as I would normally

But then decisively I should take the
Laces and the rabbit ears together
And tie them exactly as I had tied
The rabbit ears initially thusly

I have double knots on both of my boots
And could walk unhindered to Timbuktu.

It's a revelation
to discover how
much ignorance
I've been putting
up with.

A crab is a creature that looks crusty
And to be crabby is to be a drag
So why do we say that the lovely trees
Blooming along with cherry and apple

Trees but generating a deeper more
Luscious one might even say opulent
Darkly pink bordering on red flower
Why do say they are crabapple trees

Because when driving in Stillwater and
Seeing again after the bareness of
Winter the crabapple blooms unfolding
Little by little to their flowering

I feel the weight of winter dissolve with
A taste of crabapple liberation.

I'm not a bee
I don't pollinate
but winter is weighty
year after year and
blooms are liberating.

The oaks are budding after the aspen
And white paper birch with their buds being
About the size of a mouse's ear as
Jason explained while the cells are now as

Numerous as when fully grown meaning
The size of each cell will expand until
The form of the oak leaf is manifest
Signifying that the observations

Of ecologists are bringing to light
The intricacies and energies of
Life indicating that a portion of
Humanity sees beyond the trappings of

Money property and prestige and yet
Who knows what direction we are heading?

Perhaps our wisdom is
like the budding oak leaf
about the size of a
mouse's ear.

I remember a summer afternoon
When my dad gave me a bucket and a
Dandelion picker as he urged me
To expend my energy ridding the

Lawn of weeds for the colossal sum of
Five dollars which I did and even now
My mom who is over eighty years old
Is using the same picker to rid the

Lawn of weeds while now I know what the poor
Have always known that dandelions can be
Eaten and maybe I'm lazy but I've
Learned to appreciate the yellow bloom

Along with the purple Creeping Charlie
And I'm using my energy elsewise.

Perhaps my neighbors
are annoyed with me
for indulging weeds
and maybe I've found
a new way to be smug.

I haven't turned on the printing press for
Six years and I sold it about a year
And a half ago to a printer who will
Use it for parts as it's not worth very

Much and weighs over nine hundred pounds which
Maybe is why he's taken so long to
Come get it even though he said he would
So to me the obsolete machine became

A symbol of inertia sitting there
Uselessly collecting dust but about
Twenty years ago I proudly learned the
Tricks of the trade while also keeping my

Hands clean and I really took pleasure in
Listening to mechanical music.

Two big guys
with barely enough
smarts muscle
and leverage
took it away.

I was running the press when my Dad walked
Into the printing room from the garage
Just after he learned that his long-time friend
And business partner had died of pneumonia

Struggling for breath and I saw a shocked
And frightened expression on my Dad's face
Because Guy Johnson had a confidence
And common sense wisdom about him that

Balanced my Dad's more frenetic nature
And provided my Dad with a sense that
Everything was going to become OK
And I knew that on that day my Dad

Had lost an irreplaceable pillar of strength
And I saw my Dad's defenses were shattered.

On that day
my Dad's face
momentarily
expressed what
his words couldn't.

Stillwater is a hilly town and when
I leave home to do my circuit over
The Crossing Bridge into the countryside
And back again on my bicycle I

Start from the north hill to the downtown of
Stillwater but from then on I'm climbing
Until the furthermost limit of my
Ride and at the section over the bridge

High above the valley I encounter
The buffeting of a side or of a
Head wind impeding my pedaling but
When the wind is pushing me I move in

Silence absorbing the warmth of the sun
And exulting in the effortless speed.

On any given day
at some point on my
circular route the wind
challenges and
exhilarates me.

The understanding of political
Controversy is like the handling
Of the Russian dolls that hide smaller dolls
Within them with the largest doll being

The media sport of making victims
And villains with the frolic of public
Accusation that somehow overlooks
The motives of the accuser but the

Secrets of the intricacies and the
Histories of the issues involving
The interests of the politicos are
Well concealed within the receding dolls

While the hardworking citizen isn't
Aware of the thrust of malevolence.

From an idealistic
point of view the
innermost doll
represents only
questions.

I've not been going through the trouble of
Lifting the garage door and driving the
Car inside anymore as the weather
Is warmer now and the apple blossoms

Are in bloom by my driveway looking in
A glance very much like popcorn and on
The bicycle yesterday I could smell
The perfume of the flowering trees on

The avenues of Stillwater and I'd
Have to be dead not to appreciate
The explosion of white and pink blossoms
In passing while the leaves are almost grown

In contrast to the bareness of branches
Weeks ago and the leaves are so brilliant.

Even with a gray sky
with rain drops falling
this morning spring colors
are bursting with joyous
energy.

On the one hand nature appears lovely
In the shape of apple blossoms and on
The other aggressive as when buckthorn
Spreads across the country by way of the

Robins eating the buckthorn berries and
Pooping the buckthorn seeds about or the
Way sparrows were brought from England to eat
The detestable larvae infecting

The trees in the parks of New York City
With the sparrows spreading across the land
Or the way the Burmese Python is so
Dominant in the everglade grasses

Of Florida because people kept the
Pythons as pets yet somehow they got loose.

People played a part
in the invasiveness
of species yet people
are also invasively
natural.

My driving experience in Japan
Was different on a motorcycle
And a scooter as I was vulnerable
On the frenetic streets of Kyoto to

The trucks and buses and taxis as the
Japanese are accustomed to beeping
Their horns without the animosity
We Americans do as they will beep

Merely to let a driver know that they
Are present and I found myself getting
Upset as if I were quite unjustly
Being scolded and in an instant I

Became angry regardless of daily
Meditation as habit is ingrained.

People emote
differently from
place to place.

If I wrote my own obituary
Today as a service to the people
I would point out that you shouldn't pronounce
Hippopotamus slowly because if

You did others would think you were depressed
Or they may suspect you were trying to
Be funny because sincerity
Of purpose mandates that the syllables

Come out in pell-mell fashion with little
Inflection as the attention of the
Listeners should go to the creature and
Not the word — and as a further service

To humanity I would ask readers
When did you last say hippopotamus?

If a person isn't
saying hippopotamus
once in a while
it's a sign of a
cloistered life.

When moving the snow off the driveway of
My responsibility I yearn for
The overlapping appearance of the
Tulips apple trees and lilacs blooming

In a crescendo of renewing growth
In Stillwater rising into flower
With apple blossoms by my driveway
With Creeping Charlie and dandelions

Underneath with the various perfumes
Mingling about the air which must be a
Bumblebee's heaven but then after a
Day of persisting rain I see on the

Pavement and the grass under both of my
Apple trees what seems to be confetti.

The blooming and
dispersion varies from
flower tree and bush
and the parade lasts
more than a month.

I am a colossus striding about
The house with a banished ex-wife with things
Being exactly where I left them and
I am a beneficent captain with

Johnnie scampering underfoot and with
Kitcat lying upon me when I am
Sequestered on the couch deciding when
To feed them invested with the power

To turn the doorknobs and to open the
Necessary containers only this
Morning Kitcat finagled the doorknob
And suddenly they burst into the room

Jumping onto the bed rousing me from
Quietude and demanding to be fed.

Kitcat is
cleverly
dangerous
and needs to
be watched.

I am a colossus striding about
The house with a banished ex-wife with things
Being exactly where I left them and
I am a beneficent captain with

Johnnie scampering underfoot and with
Kitcat lying upon me when I am
Sequestered on the couch deciding when
To feed them invested with the power

To turn the doorknobs and to open the
Necessary containers only this
Morning Kitcat finagled the doorknob
And suddenly they burst into the room

Jumping onto the bed rousing me from
Quietude and demanding to be fed.

Kitcat is
cleverly
dangerous
and needs to
be watched.

Suddenly a flit in the air alerts
Me as I am leaving the store that the
Swallows of Walmart have retuned again
And I don't know why a strip mall attracts

Them and don't know how far they've traveled
Or whether these are the same birds of last
Year and I wonder whether their turning
Cutting and fleeting in the air as if

They were blades is joyful for them but I'm
Grateful for the openness of the sky
Even with the horizon of big box
Stores any moment as quick as lightning

As long as I am clear-headed and poised
That I may see something marvelous.

Riding my bicycle
at a certain spot along
the river I am assailed
about my ears mouth and eyes
by gnats.

Letters are tricky and capable of
Invisibility as when I typed
"Raise" when intending to type "rise" which went
Unnoticed for several days until an

Instant of recognition made me hit
Myself in the forehead with a fist as
Overlooking the obvious is what
I do and making marks upon a page

Assuming someone else will spend the time
In reading them is a presumption I
May not earn and composing poems is
Like being a trapeze artist swinging

On a rope preparing to launch myself
Into the air and hoping to be caught.

I love the spontaneity
and moment of
assertion within
communication.

Even with the east wind against me as
I'm pedaling over the Crossing Bridge
Seeing the little ripples below me
Of the wide expanse of the river I

Can imagine I'm conquering the
River and mastering the elements
Whether the day is cloudy or sunny
As hard as the wind may blow I have the

Stamina and proper gears to make it
Across absorbing the panorama
Into my being but the life-giving
Movement of water is continuous

Southwards along a valley of the earth
And I can chuckle at my presumption.

The river passes through
every living being
becomes an ocean
drifting clouds and a
creek in the woods.

When the leaves are fully grown then most of
The apples blossoms are upon the grass
And spring rain is saturating the soil
And the grass is growing voraciously

And does need to be mowed regularly
Otherwise the mower will become clogged
Making me yank on the cord to start it
Again which I'd rather not do as it

Is getting harder to start but I am
Learning to appreciate mowing the
Grass once in a week and leveling the
Creeping Charlie and the dandelions

But this year I've found I'm a little sad
When its time to mow the apple blossoms.

The annual parade
of blossoms in spring
that I anticipate
in winter is
disintegrating.

I don't get close enough to observe them
But I heard them before the leaves came out
Making a chorus of background music
Sounding continuously in the spring

And I hardly noticed until Jason
Told me what they were the little creatures
With bug eyes and squishy bodies who puff
Themselves to expel the air and announce

Their presence and aesthetically they
Are just odd and ugly enough to be
Ludicrously pleasing jumping as they
Do with springy legs and snatching insects

On the fly with their adroitness of tongues
As our children learn in their early years.

I heard the peepers
chorus and wood frogs
for many years
without awareness.

They traipse about the town in families
Strolling on the grass near the ponds and lakes
With the parents leading and the fuzzy
Newborns following in a line making

A caravan and they aren't afraid to
Cross a road and bring the traffic to a
Halt as they exhibit a confident
Dignity that projects a measure of

Distance between them and others because
The parents are irascible and will
Rush and hiss at intruders but as they
Walk they wobble because of their bulging

Bodies and ridiculously long necks
Culminating into pinched little heads.

They are aerodynamic
as the geese form themselves
into lines like arrows
slipping through the air
going distances.

On the corner of my property next
To a fire hydrant and under the
Cottonwood where the city snowplows are
Misjudging the distance and tearing up

The grass for year after year there are my
Lilac bushes that I look forward to
As a gage of season recalling them
In the snow-bourn depth of February

Because the lilac blossoms are the last
Celebration of spring and the gateway
Into summer marking when the roots of
The grass and the bushes and the trees are

Busy drinking water and minerals
And the leaves are absorbing the sunlight.

My ex-wife planted the
lilacs and they have only
one scent but it's pleasing
they come in three shades
of purple.

The pandemic didn't interrupt the
Accusatory words of politics
But only served to deepen divisions
Of America along party lines

As patriotism separated
Into warring factions a while ago
And presently the arguments concern
Who is to blame for which delinquency

As the nation is reopening for
Business by various degrees in each
Of the fifty states as everyone is
Encouraged to wear a mask in public

And to maintain six feet of distance from
Each other as contagion continues.

Public discourse is
at such a pitch of
acrimony it's hard
to guess what could
unify the nation.

There is a lawyer named Jim
Who managed the FBI
He lied to Congress
And lied on TV
And thinks he's a marvelous guy.

There is a lawyer named Bill
Who directs the DOJ
He's smart as a fox
And follows the law
And Jim is finally going to pay.

America is
celebrating
Memorial Day
for the nation's
soldiers killed
in battle as the
roots of summer
are beginning to
drink water
and minerals.

— *Tekkan*

Everyday Mind VX

Puffs of dandelion seeds
little white spheres
scattered across the lawn
rising above the grass
are ready to go.

I got tired of watching the riders on
Fancy high-tech bicycles pass me by
So I purchased one with the stimulus
Money the government sent because of

The pandemic and on my first day I
Was going twice as fast only I have
To be careful in downtown Stillwater
Where people saunter around on foot and

Where I have to stop at the traffic lights
Because I'm using clip-on pedals and
Shoes that cost over a hundred dollars
And I am having fun zipping about but

Haven't got the hang of getting out of
The pedals so I brake and fall over.

Sitting at my desk
this morning I'm twisting
my ankle in pedal
disengagement mode
practicing.

For March April and May the barbershops
Have been closed because of the pandemic
Virus and they're opening on Monday
And thank God because the state of my hair

Is deplorable and I realize
On the scale of tragedy the weight of
Unappealing hair is wafer thin but
I want a return to normalcy and

And the persistent isolation of
Social distancing not allowing for
Conversation or for non-essential
Commerce is reaching the limit of its

Practicability and people are
Going to wig out if it doesn't end soon.

I've very tempted
to run the clipper
over my head but
I'm hesitant to
create divots.

In a chilly interlude within the
Warmer days of summer I noticed a
Blur in the air while mowing the grass that
With a more discerning attention turned

Out to be a dragonfly zigzagging
As only a dragonfly is able
With its four wings maneuvering forward
And backward and up and down and stopping

Suddenly and hovering in the air
Knowing as I do that a dragonfly has
Spherical eyes absorbing everything
About itself which makes me grateful that

I am not a fruit fly exposed to the
Predation of a true flying dragon.

Sunny summer brightness
goes very well with
the neon incandesce
of a dragonfly.

The onset of the pandemic virus
Three months ago forcing businesses to
Close and people to put their lives on hold
Was followed last week by the brutal and

Unjustified killing of a black man
By a white policeman prompting peaceful
Protests during the days and furious
Riots and lootings during the nights and

Americans are confused and angry
And divided with our major cities
Despoiled and burning with long simmering
Animosities igniting into

Warring factions with national guardsmen
Girding for a forceful intervention.

Society is revealed
as idealistic with
civilizing
institutions
sedately founded
upon latent volcanoes.

The video of a white policeman
Kneeling on the neck of a black man and
Killing him was a spark inflaming the
Outrage of Americans who believe

After all there is no racial justice
In America leading to a week
Of rioting and looting throughout the
Nation — and videos of black-garbed and

Masked thugs beating to unconsciousness the
Passersby or storeowners defending
Their property are broadcast once the sun
Goes down with darkness encouraging the

Violence of thugs that is always just
Around the corner and seeking an excuse.

Equality before the
law and justice are precious
American ideals
worthy of enforcing
in difficult times.

Early in the afternoon yesterday
A new humidity was in the air
With a haze obscuring a view of the
Distance southwards of the river valley

And the sun was beating on my arms as
I was clipped into the pedals pumping
My legs steadily pacing the incline
To the Crossing Bridge gripping the lower

Curls of the bicycle handles learning
To shift to the proper gear maintaining
My exertion at eighty percent of
Capacity aware of the dark clouds

Of an impending thunderstorm coming
With gusts from the northeast behind me.

This morning a
million drops of dew
are sparkling in the grass
with the rising sun.

The shards of conflicting opinions and
Passions have erupted into chaos
In cities with rioters destroying
Businesses and battling the police

And so many have a reason why the
Violence is necessary either
To address longstanding injustices
Or to defend lifetimes of effort while

Livelihoods and families are on the
Line as the opposing attitudes are
Hardening into concrete and voices
Of moderation are overwhelmed and

Will we find a resolution of our
Confusion or a just a simmering mess?

Certainly lies are
being told and politics
is a driving force but
who's to blame is
contestable.

It's not only the white peonies and
Dew drops on the grass that are worthy of
Celebrating this morning it's also
The sunlight that when I'm closing my eyes

And enjoying the quiet I'm noticing
The warmth of the sun inside my body
I'm seeing my eyelids are filtering
The light into the brightest shade of red

And I can pinpoint how high the sun is
As its rising by the intensity
Of it's heat giving me a sensation
To go with a perception of the peace

And I don't have to do anything or
To please anyone to earn the quiet.

Sensing the sun through my
closed eyelids enjoying
the heat radiating I
imagine myself a
tomato.

The splendor of our summer days presents
A face of reality I'd like to
Enjoy forever when the sun is a
Power browning my skin with its touch and

Warming the inside of my body and
When we can sleep with cool breezes with the
Windows open and on awakening
We can listen to the birds permeate

The air with song but soon mosquitoes will
Be biting and the humidity will
Be sweltering and the smallest tick is
Capable of imparting Lyme disease

And even as the roots of trees and grass
Are busy a barren season will come.

The face of reality
is like a weaving
of smoke
endlessly
fascinating.

As I'm sitting in the lotus posture
Quietly and with energy coursing
Through my body the assertion of a
Vigorous wind in the leaves becomes a

Dharma gate of curiosity as
I can hear the weight of injustice and
Cruelty in the mournful expression
Of the wind as if sorrowful questions

And grief are mixing in the blusters of
The leaves and the questions are unanswered
And I hear a lamentation in the
Wind rising upward to a crescendo

Of intensity and dissipating
Into surrendering despondency.

And yet there is also
consolation and
quiet within
the voices of the
wind in the leaves.

There is talk in our meetings about the
People in Wisconsin who aren't wearing
Masks and who are gathering in groups and
Are not keeping a safe distance between

Each other while we Minnesotans are
Seeing and hearing each other online
Within little boxes on screens with some
Of us scolding don't they know they can have

The virus without its symptoms spreading
It to vulnerable loved ones but I
Am enjoying the sun after such a
Chilly spring and I can close my eyes and

Know exactly where it is by its heat
Feeling a little dizzy and peaceful.

Pandemic virus
protests in cities
riots in cities with
most of us wearing
masks.

We got news from the United Nation's
World Health Organization that it is
Not likely that people with the virus
Without the symptomatic sneezing or

Coughing are in fact infecting other
People which undercuts the reasons why
Our leaders issued stay-at-home orders
And strangled our so-called nonessential

Businesses and shuttered the nation's schools
Which have never happened before and yet
Never mind it's only one opinion
Among many as no one knows for sure

And it's better safe than sorry except
For those whose livelihoods were destroyed.

Some of us can shrug
and laugh and others
can't while some are
getting sick and
dying.

The sky today is white like the pages
Of a book of poetry and in its
Whiteness is the essence of the oceans
And of waterfalls and springs in the way

Of metamorphoses and along the
Margins of the sky there are the millions
Of green leaves tossing in a wind with wind
And leaves cooperating and stirring

Crescendos of lyrical music that
Not everyone will notice but for those
Who listen the soundings are homilies
Consoling and soothing and there are no

Words embodied in the sky or in the
Meaning of the boisterous leafy wind.

The white pages of a
book of poetry are
full of words but the
words point beyond
the poetry.

I tap a finger on a key and a
Letter appears on the whiteness of the
Screen and the whiteness of the screen is like
The emptiness from which everything comes

And in the beginning there are spasms
Of thoughts that aren't cohering into a
Pattern worthy of expression as I
Put my chin on the heel of my hand while

Looking at the white of the screen waiting
For a direction that may bloom into
An inspiration that may form into
A poem that perhaps communicates

Something specific and meaningful to
Whomever may be reading it later.

But emptiness really
isn't white or black
and emptiness and
emanation come
together.

They have buckteeth that are propitious
For chewing wood and they like to climb and
Loiter in the trees making good use of
Their prehensile tails and if ever an

Animal could become a metaphor
For a period of history these
Are the creatures that serve the purpose as
When waddling along the ground they look

As inoffensive and vulnerable
As a squirrel or a rabbit but don't
Be so hasty as to venture a bite
Because they are extremely prickly

And you might find your snout impaled with
The needles and barbs of a porcupine.

Given the polarized
nature of America's
politics the porcupine
could serve as the nation's
emblem.

The days of life are like the layering
Of pages with the white of the paper
Being the light of possibility
And whoever notices the whiteness

And reliability of paper
Pages one following another as
Natural and as binding as the days
Of life as the substance of the paper

Was once the living trees absorbing the
Sunlight and drinking the water and the
Minerals of the soil as the whiteness
Of the paper is a reflection of

Sunlight and can you close your eyes over
The open pages and feel the sun's warmth?

There's a kinship between
the pages of my life
and the cottonwood
by my house flowing
in the wind.

In any room if one listens there is
A hum of electricity on the
Tipping point of consciousness as it takes
A ceasing of thoughts and a quietude

Of activity to hear the constant
Operation of machines channeling
Energy lighting our rooms cooling or
Heating space refrigerating our food

And in the distance there are power plants
Utilizing coal or natural gas
Or uranium marshaling a flow
Of electrical juice through a network

Of power lines crossing America
And into every solitary home.

We live like Kings
and yet through the
habit of comparison
we find reasons for
envy.

The elements of society are
Tensed and fractured into factions and the
News is a brew of shootings and riots
And accusatory narratives as

Ideals of justice and law enforcement
Are disintegrating as people are
Hating people who believe or who look
Different from them as the media

And politicos are spewing hateful
Words as they are whipping and driving the
Masses who they have hypnotized into
Fury surpassing moderation or

Introspection into a concoction
Of political opportunity.

One has to be wary
or belligerent to
express opinions
different from
the dominate narratives.

The riots and the pandemic are symptoms
Of human volatility and who
Could have predicted in December the
Cancellation of major league baseball

With owners and players disagreeing
On how to price a short season but I'm
Getting up early and applying the
Method of persistency crossing my

Legs and meditating in the midst of
Uncertainty and this morning I saw
Five almost identical crows cawing
And strutting together on my lawn and

When I stepped outside they scattered to the
Trees harshly complaining of my presence.

The blooms of pink roses
by my patio in the
morning light of June
are evidence of
continuity.

All the leaves have lost their springtime luster
The apple and lilac blossoms are gone
The resonance of the wind and the leaves
Is much less noticeable when it's hot

The heat is slowing the growth of the grass
And the afternoon sun is bearing down
Making the shade under the leaves welcome
And instead of the purple flowering

Of the Creeping Charlie the white blossoms
Of clover are predominant now and
The stems of little oval leaves and thorns
That are so easy to pass without thought

Are blooming within the humidity
In a collection of lovely roses.

Pink roses and
blooming clover
appear with the
summer heat
at my home.

An Ode to My Mentor — Cid Corman

By an old oak in Pioneer Park I
Discovered a stone on the ground that I
Absentmindedly picked up and handled
Turning it about until I noticed

A curve of it abutted my fleshy
Part below my thumb and another curve
Fit snugly within the cup of my hand
And it was small and round enough for my

Fingers to fold over the stone resting
My fingertips on the only flat part
Of the stone and there even happened to
Be a place for the tip of my pinky

Finger to rest — this random stone is a
Perfect match for the inside of my hand.

Holding the stone
warming the stone
imagining holding hands
I feel comprehended.

Kitcat lets me know when he's wanting the
Container of dry cat food that I keep
In the microwave by jumping onto
The microwave and pawing at a framed

Painting hanging above it and sometimes
He knocks the painting down so I'm compelled
To present the container to him in
The bathroom separate from Johnnie who

Isn't allowed the dry food and after
Kitcat is finished eating he pounds on
The door and yowls and I let him out
And then he rushes out — but as soon as

I put the container back inside the
Microwave he paws the painting again.

As Kitcat goes back
for a second helping
I suspect he's getting
a kick out of
bossing me around.

Summer Solstice

A cottonwood puff is rising in a breeze
And an eagle is skimming a crosswind
A lower cloud is moving northward while
The higher clouds are slowly going south

I heard numerous birds through the window
This morning in between my rising and
Dissipating thoughts and there was a dog
Barking in the distance and touching my

Ears but my mind kept returning to the
Accusatory currents of thoughts that
Are ricocheting across the Internet
Charging and countercharging racism

And I'm trying not to set what I think
Against what others believe I should think.

A poet said the great way
isn't difficult for
those who do not
pick and choose.

Sitting quietly without moving on
The grass he could be mistaken for a
Bumpy sort of rock but with a closer
View his squatting posture is apparent

And he looks like something that you wouldn't
Want to step on and mess your shoe with but
With a more careful look you can see his
Bulging eyes and his pudgy body and

He really is a funny-looking thing
Although his impassive face does bespeak
A degree of dignity and yet when
He flings himself forward with his springy

Rear legs he is so ridiculous
You wonder how this creature came to be.

I have outgrown
my childish urges
to grab and squish
a toad.

I do feel a little sorry for plants
Because they have so few choices to make
Passively accepting whatever comes
Sure they can extend their roots and flower

But they prosper or not depending on
Which side of the shady hill the seed falls
And on the consistency of the rain and
The sun and the minerals of the soil

And on the temperature — even so
There is a noble tenacity and
A splendid variety to behold
That with an intelligent pruning can

Produce an exquisite combination
Of thorns and irresistible beauty.

A red rose is as
iconic as the sun
and the moon.

Jason's Alternative View:

Plants create the hills the shade the living
Soil the carbon cycle the atmosphere
And the climate as they influence the
Starting and ending of the ice ages

Spreading their propagules throughout the earth
Choosing where and where not to germinate
In the conditions in which they can thrive
With orchid seeds and botrychium fern

Spores traveling in the jet stream to all
The corners of creation as the plants
Operate in a fundamentally
Different time frame than humans — which is

Their superpower their consciousness and
Their total planetary influence.

Plants use an abundance
of choice teaching us
to align ourselves with
the reality of our
cosmic incarnation.

(My friend Jason is an ecologist.)

Over fifteen years it has happened that
If I'm lying on my left side sleeping
I could wake any day with my left ear
Plugged with wax and because it happens so

Infrequently I muddle through pulling
On my earlobe extending my pinky
Fingertip down into my ear as far
As I can or tilting my head just so

In the shower to let the warm water
Stream directly into my ear canal
And it happens on the verge of panic
That the congealed wax will pop and my

Hearing is magically restored so
Then I can forget it ever happened.

But last night the wax
was determinedly
congealed and the
extension of panic
was lengthy.

A conflagration is spreading within
The big cities of America with
Mobs pulling down and dismembering the
Statues of statesmen as the mob isn't

Interested in the minutiae
Of history but they are inspired
With revolutionary fever to
Destroy American history and

Construct a radically different
Nation while the police are ordered to
Do nothing because the governors where
It's happening are accumulating

Political advantage from the mayhem
As a tacit way of attacking foes.

Using the leverage
of violent mobs is
as unpredictable
as lighting a grass fire
during a drought.

I don't want to argue with people who
Have different political views from
Me and yet because I cherish points of
View in opposition to others in

A time of conflagration I gather
The information to justify my
Reasoning being aware that I am
Cultivating passions and obsessing

Over the consequences of defeat
And victory immersing myself in
Battles without end and realizing
Humans have a way of painstakingly

Constructing a house of cards and in a
Pique of fury burning it to the ground.

In meditation I
pivot precariously
on the point of letting go
of thoughts and listening to
birds.

Now that the wax has been flushed from my ears
I can hear the sound of the rain within
My semi-consciousness and sleep and there
Is the kind of thunder that I haven't

Heard for years but a thunderous night is
An experience that one can never
Really forget and with every booming
Vibration there is an arching bolt of

Lightning illuminating a strange and
Ominous landscape full of tension and
Fear that I can only glimpse and every
Thundering impact is unique making

A dramatic but fleeting impression
In between the pattering of the rain.

The spattering of the
rain outlasts the
violence in the air
immersing anxiety
within a lullaby.

My clogs are much too big for my feet but
As long as I'm not walking in tall grass
And exposed to ticks and Lyme disease they are
The perfect form of summer shoe because

They have high heels and provide three inches
Of additional height and I don't have to
Bend over to tie a lace but just to
Slip into and out of them and on a whim

At my desk I can instantly achieve
Nakedness all the way up to my short
Pants while kneading the carpet with my toes
And yet when walking around town I am

Protected from bits of glass and gritty
Sand — striding about profoundly happy.

Only in summer
are my heels and ankles
and most of my feet
almost completely
liberated.

The roundness of a watermelon is
Challenging because it's slippery and
Hard to hold stationary with one hand
While cutting through the stubborn rind with the

Other but I'm clever so I put the
Watermelon inside the sink and use
The hole of the drain as a centering
Device that allows me to lustily

Saw into it with my watermelon
Knife that has very large and wicked teeth
And I don't have attend so much to
What my other hand is doing but I

Do find that the sides of the sink are an
Impediment to free-flowing motion.

Cutting off the tip of
my thumb I realize
I do have to attend
to what my other
hand is doing.

I have to overcome my resistance
To getting out of bed and wait until
The drowsiness of sleep dissipates but
Then I get to experience one of

The joys of living when my ideas
Start to pop like a bag of popcorn in
A microwave oven when I get to
Discover what was important about

What happened yesterday and how I feel
About a conversation and there are
Always words worth my pondering and then
I turn my attention to today and

Consider what I want to do and then
My energetic optimism comes.

I used to be so inside
of my thoughts that
I was blind to the
quality of my thoughts and
they ran away with me.

I am jubilant to see it on the
Way to Hudson as I'm driving over
The rise of a hill appearing with a
Cornfield and pasture next to a house a

Cattle barn and a corn silo and it
Doesn't look like it belongs there as its
Slender leaves are streaming in the wind as
It seems not only receptive but to be

The source of the wind and not merely to
Reflect but to emanate the sunlight
Standing out within its orderly and
Prosaic surroundings with its easy

Rippling and whispering in the wind as
A flaunting and flourishing touch of grace.

I forget all about it
until I crest the hill and
am captured again
in quiet celebration
of the willow tree.

I remembered the story of the Zen
Master who asked the monk — what is it that
Comes to talk to me — and the monk paused and
Then he turned and walked away because he

Could not answer the riddling question
And he knew that the master would ask
Until he had a satisfactory
Reply and I remembered the master's

Question as I was walking away from
My friends after our conversation as
They were continuing to listen and
To speak and I asked myself what is it

That comes and goes and listens and speaks and
Wherever it goes the world is changing?

And there is always
more going on
in every direction
than can possibly be
comprehended.

In every day at any time of the
Day and it's especially true when the
Summer heat is lingering through the night
And into the morning and sapping my

Energy that there does happen to be
A little listlessness to be managed
And if not managed could well become a
Pool of apathy to wallow within

But I can close my eyes when facing the
Sun and see my eyelids turn red with the
Sunlight and I can linger within the
Heat of the sunlight and listen to the

Hum of electricity in the room
And then there is only me and the sun.

Dazzling energy
penetrates my red eyelids
apart from notions
of urgency making me
just a little dizzy.

I saw a busy little bumblebee
Bobbing about the clover of my grass
Within a carefree summer afternoon
And it really wasn't entirely

Without care as I had to mow the grass
And whack the grass around the rock gardens
And pick up the twigs my cottonwood drops
And spray some herbicide on pesky weeds

But once I begin bumbling about
Doing one thing after another does
Become a moving and a merging of
Mindless activity and so I feel

That the bee and me are simpatico
Following a simple program of chores.

I wonder what the bee
is thinking as my
thoughts are busy with
trivialities.

The prank of slathering words on a screen
And finagling each word to cohere
Into a packet of clarity that
May survive to decorate the pages

Of a book doesn't come as simply as
It appears as the perpetual state
Of my mind resembles a Mexican
Jumping Bean of chaotic random thoughts

And it's propitious to pause enough
To permit the right word to penetrate
And settle in a proper arrangement
Somewhat like old-fashioned photography

As the camera needs a long exposure
To propound a poetic palaver.

A calico cat
leaped onto my lap
in the middle of
this poem.

It is a presidential election
Year and I have only to turn on the
Radio while driving for five minutes
To hear excited voices disputing

A current controversy to be caught
Again in the furious world of us
Versus them — whereas I had come from a
Moment in the park where I saw a bird

Flitting and coasting through the air and I
Also heard it cheeping as it flew and
The sky was as clear and blue as could be
With only a crescent moon to be seen

As the leaves were lit by the rising sun
And bird song punctuated the breezes.

I have perfect freedom
to navigate between
the stridency of
humanity or
evanescence.

I don't agree with the snobs who think that
The plastic flamingos that people in
Minnesota sprinkle their yards with are
Crass or gaudy because the color pink

Is incandescent and goes very well
With a summer afternoon when the blue
Of the sky and the white of the clouds and
The green of the grass are all shining with

The nourishing sun and it's true that the
Form of a synthetic flamingo or
A flock of plastic flamingos aren't on
A par with Michelangelo's David

But the audacity and flamboyance
Of hosting pink flamingos is worthy.

The flamingos are
a tonic to the eyes
and a taste of the
exotic.

Do you feel the momentum in the air
In the month of July when the sun is
Burning the air with its touch and all the
Leaves are receptive and drinking in the

Radiance as if the trees were sailing
Ships with every sail aloft and full of
The force of the wind and the fire of the
Orb is penetrating stimulating

And scorching the skin and the blue of the
Sky is overwhelmed with the pulsation
Of descending heat and every kind of
Flower is in kaleidoscopic bloom

And the shade under the trees is welcome
As an oasis from the blazing sun?

A white t-shirt
becomes a blazing
emblem of
summer frolic
and liberation.

Some of us stubbornly believe somewhere
Out in the woods there is the disheveled
Giant that we dub with the sobriquet
Big Foot and he is a shy and slippery

Fellow almost always evading our
Scientific verification and
He surely possesses a prodigious
Intellect otherwise how could he have

Eluded an eager hunter's bullet
For all these years and I have considered
Having seen the one grainy snippet of
A video of him striding away

Swinging his arms that he could do with a
Vigorous combing out of ticks and fleas.

I've been told that
we don't find any
Big Foot residue
because porcupines
eat his bones.

Once the gyms were closed in the spring because
Of the pandemic I had to find a
Different way of exercising and
The simplest method is to lift the

Weight of my body as if I were a
Dumbbell so I started doing sit-ups
And push-ups hundreds of times and it is
Frustrating because my mind wanders and

I lose count of the repetitions so
How many I do are probably more
Or less than I think I've done and in the
Process it's amazing where my mind will

Wander as I am becoming obsessed
With the supreme importance of my toes.

Did you know
when doing push-ups
the tiny tips of big toes
become essential
balancing points?

My laser printer needs an adjustment
As every now and then it will run through
Two sheets of paper instead of one and
I regret the waste of paper but not

Enough to hire someone to fix it and
So I use the curved sheets that cannot be
Processed through the printer again without
Jamming as notepaper for writing down

The spelling of names or for the exact
Wording of phrases or to record an
Instant inspiration for a poem
And I am writing many notes on each

Single sheet of paper and the pile of
Paper is slowly accumulating.

I look at the pile of
clean and exactly cut
sheets of paper ready for
use as the epitome
of civilization.

I haven't run out of surprising things
To see this summer as everywhere I'm
Driving wildflowers and hydrangeas are
Catching my eye as luscious accent points

In my day and I can't calculate how
Many years I've wasted attending to
A crazy monologue in my head and
Sometimes there are two of me debating

Fractious controversies devolving to
Indecision and all the while beyond
My thinking there is a festival to
Be experienced bearing down on me

From every direction meeting me more
Than halfway and ready to transform me.

I live in a cosmos
of supernovas
of black holes
of wildflowers
of hydrangeas.

The leaves are not themselves complete without
The sunlight radiating upon them
And the blue of the atmosphere is not
An item existing by itself but

The atmosphere is a co-creator
With the earth and the sun and the oceans
And I don't believe the boundary of
My skin separates me from the swirl of

Life as every breath is an exchange of
Essence and I popped into consciousness
Not making any distinctions about
Distances and I could very well have

Reached my hands upward to possess the moon
To become mystified by its presence.

I didn't invent these words
but I am playing with them
and am playing at
understanding.

It was a surprising observation
Once the car was going on the highway
To see a tree frog plastered onto the
Windshield resisting the force of the wind

With its toes splayed on the glass and body
A study of stoic resolution
For what was it to do otherwise than
To hold on for dear life and so the frog

Became an emblem of anyone who
Is caught without warning in perilous
Circumstances impelled forward to an
Unknown destination leaving behind

Comfortable familiarity
And straining every fiber to stay put.

It's astounding
such a puny
squishy creature
with bug eyes
has so much pluck.

What does a cornfield extending into
The distance with an empty sky on
The horizon mean to you if you stop
To question it — and there is often a

Line of coniferous trees sheltering
A homestead from the wind in the country —
However far one looks there is always
A boundary of the sky and the earth —

On occasion a wisp of cloud becomes
Visible — do you take the time to watch
It blow and change its shape — you may see the
Pace of metamorphosis if you do —

Even the emptiness of the sky is
Tricky as it's really filled with sunlight.

No eyes / no sun
no ears / no rain
no skin / no coolness
no nose / no roses
no tongue / no watermelon
no mind / then what?

To be and to spread its leaves every year
Sedately growing on a limestone bluff
Overlooking downtown Stillwater and
Set high above the wide flowing river

The oak is reaching upwards to the sun
Growing acorns and spreading its branches
Expanding its girth in every season
Its roots drinking minerals and water

It was growing when the American
Frontier passed by and a lumber baron
Built a mansion next to it but now the
Building is gone while it is flourishing

There used to be steamboats on the river
And lumberjacks came into town for fun.

The oak adds a touch of
majesty to its home
in Pioneer Park on
the northwards bluff of
Stillwater Minnesota.

Memory is weighty before the dawn
When I'm weary and reluctant to move
When my mind is busy remembering
My marriage and my rambunctious children

When there was so much living yet to do
With so many things to look forward to
And with decades of possibility
But now I have my cats for company

As my kids are pursuing their own dreams
And I would rather let the memories
Go but it's apparent that how I am
Remembering is beyond my control

In the early hours of the morning
When I feel the weight of what has happened.

I enjoy energy
listening to birds
through the window
while meditating
in the morning.

Before I bought a racing bicycle
I was riding a clunker and had to
Watch in frustration as other riders
With better bikes would pass me by but now

When a rider is bold enough to pass
Then he becomes a rabbit whom I chase
And I don't want to catch him because then
I would become the rabbit but what I

Want is to prove to myself that I can
Follow the best of them up the steepest
Hill or along a rising gradient
Against the wind and I've been successful

With the guys with fancy jerseys and bikes
Until I encountered Doug from the gym.

Doug is a
knowledgeable
modest friendly
smiling fellow who
left me far behind.

Yes we're in the latter half of July
And even though the light is sparkling in
The cottonwood leaves well into evening
I'm beginning to notice a mellow

Golden touch about the sunlight and I
Also saw while driving around town my
First sightings of the paling of the green
Leaves into shadings of red and yellow

And maybe I'm falling into a mood
And looking for reasons to be gloomy
As year after year I've trained myself to
Specify the descent into winter

While I could enjoy the open windows
And cool mornings and the hot afternoons.

There is always a tinge
of February in
Minnesota — light in
July but harsh in
March April and May.

I enjoy an hour of sanctuary
At my desk for playing with words apart
From the madness of current events as
Vitriol and accusation is out

Of control with riots continuing
For two months in Portland while dozens of
People are being shot every weekend
In Chicago as children are being

Killed in homes and cars by the stray bullets
Involved in gang warfare and parental
Heartbreak is useful for fabricating
Political narratives but the threads

Of societal disease are tangled
Almost beyond honest comprehension.

It's much easier
to specify an enemy
to foment a rage
to seek advantage
than to comprehend.

I was walking on a cool afternoon
And entered the grounds of a neighborhood
Temple in Kyoto when no one else was
About and I came upon the bell and

I held the beam hanging on a chain and
I swung the beam backward and forward and
Struck the bell and the sound resonated
In the air slowly and deeply and I

Felt the vibration pulsating within
My ears and the reverberation was
Continuous in somber crests and troughs
And I've never heard anything like it

And I don't completely understand it
But it sounded both solemn and joyful.

I might say the
temple bell continues
to reverberate as a
summons on a
threshold.

I would rather not be an amateur
Psychologist especially when it
Comes to deciphering the behavior
Of my cat but I can't tolerate the

Odor of cat urine when entering
My home and I've met him more than halfway
Provided him with another litter
Box taking me twice the time for cleaning

Yet he seems to delight in peeing not
Inside but all around the litter box
And things can't continue as they are as
I'd be ashamed to bring home visitors

Yet moral exhortation wouldn't work
When Kitcat is incapable of shame.

I admit a little
observation goes
a long way as the
litter box is too little
and Kitcat is too big.

I scatter poems about me printing
Copies and forgetting where I leave them
And my Mom came upon the previous
Poem and in alarm she provided

Me with cleaning canisters and strongly
Discouraged the publication of the
Poem and I accepted the supplies
And thanked her but she doesn't know that I've

Already read the poem to several
Friends and have given and received just what
I wanted — a laugh — and this morning I
Received the continuing expression

Of my mother's concern and affection
And that's an inspiration for today.

Kitty residue
is manageable
but a mother's love
is indestructible.

My Mom has always been good at growing
Plants inside the house taking care to find
A fitting placement with a sufficient
Amount of sunshine for each of them and

Outside she exercises a distaste
For dandelions by patrolling the
Lawn with a bucket and picker even
Though she is over eighty years old and

The home and property where my siblings
And I were raised and where our children and
Even their children are visiting will
Be remembered as a sanctuary

Of love in the form of geraniums
Of pansies marigolds and yellow bells.

Santa Barbara
Bemidji Galveston
Oxford and Kyoto
were my temporary
domiciles but not
home.

Each of my poems is following a
Formula by launching a miniature
Narrative and I am intending to
Intrigue and ensnare my readers with my

Initial words compelling them to press
Forward and it's a game to engender
Expectations using ordinary
Words and everyday experience in

Unusual ways and it's a riot
In the middle to change directions as
If the reader suddenly comes upon
A turning without a clue about what's

Around the corner and then I have a
Big laugh by delivering a punch line.

The truth is I often start
writing with vague ideas
not knowing where
I'm going or how
to get there.

I keep the rock that fits perfectly in
My hand upon my desk and hold it in
My palm and appreciate its weight and
Solid substance and with my fingertips

I evaluate its roundness and smooth
Texture and I raise it to my nostrils
With both of my hands and inhale to smell
Just the slightest scent of what may be

The essence of the stone or of perhaps
The lingering scent of the soil and I
Press it against my cheek as another
Way of touching it and realize that

The stone and I are fellow travelers
Coincidentally brought together.

Both of us will return
To soil but the rock will
More stubbornly preserve
its form.

Is there a word or a phrase that captures
The background of things that includes yet goes
Beyond the shade of a maple tree and
The interweaving of its branches and

Leaves that I mean resembles the sunlight
The atmosphere and even the cosmos
But is bigger than that because it does
Encompass the process of becoming

On the scale of geologic time or
The momentary transformation of
A cloud and in which every perception
And emotion I might have within a

Conversation plays its part — is there a
Word or a phrase that contains everything?

In all directions
everything is
transforming
and it's happening
now.

By practicing a steady cadence on
My bicycle without straining I can
Overcome a headwind and I enjoy
The swallows flitting from the overpass

Beyond the bridge and the killdeer startled
By my passage at the top of the hill
While further on by fields of soybeans and
Corn I notice monarch butterflies and

Grasshoppers and yellow moths and when I
Turn about for home I can rely on
A swelling slope of purple thistles to
Cheer me on and then I take a purely

Superfluous loop around a parking
Lot to listen to the chirping insects.

Sun-drenched
afternoons and
simple carefree
sweaty exertion
is glorious.

It's a relief not to be arguing
Anymore and bearing the burden that
Comes with a marriage that wasn't working
For decades and I am adapting to

The solitude of living by myself
Not having to inhibit or adjust
My behavior for another person's
Presence while I am communicating

With my cats more frequently than not with
Nonverbal exclamations that they seem
To understand yet I'm discovering
The importance of conversation with

My friends providing the give and take of
Perspectives — keeping my spirit supple.

Kitcat and I took naps
Saturday afternoon
on our backs
with our limbs
stretched carelessly.

Scientists are learning more about the
Dynamics of the event horizons
Of black holes but I don't suppose they are
Concerned about the moment happening

Now and its connection with what is called
Consciousness that can be separated
Into bits for analysis such as
Sensation and association and

Memory and volition but for me
Happiness depends upon my poise in
The moment enabling me to see
Without distraction the motion within

Oak leaves caused by excitable squirrels
While clouds are quickly moving to the south.

Is
consciousness
inside
the
moment
or
is
the
moment
inside
consciousness?

My Apple mouse stopped working because its
Cord got frayed so I traipsed to Office Max
For a replacement and discovered a
Cordless version providing untethered

Freedom of movement to go along with
The instant spell check that I'm used to and
There's a roller on top of the mouse that
Enables me to raise and lower the

Essays I'm reading online and I'm pleased
Beyond my expectations of the things
I can do with my fingertips and yet
Wherever I go and whatever I

Do on the Internet I'm still engaged
With the same old squabbling humanity.

Twenty years from now
the pile of words composed
above will become
gibberish except for
the bit about people.

I have upon my desk a replica
Version of "Sting" the small sword that Frodo
Carried into Mordor and I have the
Curved blade that Aragon was given in

Lothlorien by the queen of the elves
Galadriel and I know from reading
Tolkien that both of these weapons were forged
In the hidden kingdom of Gondolin

In the First Age of Middle Earth before
It was betrayed and destroyed by dragons
And demons and yet the blades survived to
Carry on into the War of the Rings

In the Third Age of Men when Frodo threw
The One Ring into the fire of Mount Doom.

Blades are passé
compared with
stealth airplanes
intercontinental
missiles and
battlefield lasers.

Dear Reader I'm sorry I played a trick
On you in the previous pages by
Implying that words are capable of
Containing anything other than mere

Ideas because the best that I can
Do is to point a shaky finger in
The correct general direction of
Something tangible in the real world but

You by yourself are responsible for
Making the leap of realization
Based on your own experience bearing
Upon your sincerity of purpose

Depending on your curiosity
Believing there is something to be known.

And yet straining and
staring to discover
something that's just
beyond grasping is
self-defeating.

I asked whether consciousness is inside
The moment or whether the moment is
Inside consciousness but perhaps those are not
Propitious questions as there may not

Be an inside or outside quality
Appropriate to the questions and it's
Better to believe that consciousness and
The moment arise together and then

Dissolve without each other and perhaps
They aren't separate things at all but are
One phenomenon which to me becomes
An optimistic point of view because

The implication is that consciousness
Continues beyond personality.

Is it possible
to imagine
the absence of
the moment
and consciousness?

My consciousness was occupied with an
Unpleasant dilemma last night on the
Verge of falling asleep as I became
Aware of a mosquito whining near

And far from my ear as I attempted to
Swat it but only hit my ear and I
Turned on the light but couldn't see it and
I remembered Jason's advice after

A similar incident to let it
Bite and I attempted to do so but
The resulting tension kept me from sleep
Waiting for a sting that didn't come as

I would rather have been thinking about
Anything else but I couldn't escape.

My consciousness
and the mosquito's
consciousness
were at
cross-purposes.

I gave an outside thermometer to
My father twenty years ago as a
Christmas gift with the image of the King
Of Rock n' Roll the crooner with the leer

The tousled hair and the gyrating hips
And Elvis was slouching in a golden
Suit and shirt and tie and he was even
Wearing golden shoes as a deserving

Celebration of his one hundred ten
Gold Records appearing as I supposed
The symbol of the initiation
Of the destruction of American

Culture and ever since the days of the
King the whole damn country has gone to Hell.

I suppose I'll take
the thermometer
out of its cardboard and
plastic wrappings and
use it myself.

I'm wearing a wide-brim straw hat as a
Shield from the sun and the weave of it is
Porous allowing many specks of light
To pass when the sun emerges from the

Clouds and the sky is a panoply of
Airy visions this morning as a bank
Of clouds high in the distance is fringed with
Sun looking like a heavenly mountain

But with a glance away and back again
I see predominantly gray clouds with
Feathery white edges and with rays of
The light visible and seeing the sweep

Of the sky I think the clouds are moving
Eastward but later I'm supposing north.

An occasional
clearing of the clouds
lights the brim of my hat
with brilliance.

The danger in playing with words is that
One could easily become serious
About it when going to poetry
Workshops and subjecting one's prize object

Of creativity to scrutiny
When everyone in turn can have a say
About whether an image works or a
Phrase could have been stronger or perhaps the

Use of enjambment is discordant but
I participate because I want to
Know whether my listeners or readers
Are actually understanding me

Because like trapeze artists we poets
Like to take leaps and hope that we are caught.

A bruised ego
along with a
playful attitude
is fertile ground.

There is such a big difference between
Reading the poem silently on a
Page to oneself and hearing the poem
Read by the poet and having only

Vibrations of sound to go by as the
Eye will be measuring the poem in
The form of words and lines and taking the
Luxury to linger and look deeper

While when listening to a poem the
Significance of the breaking and turning
Of the lines disappears and the rhythm
And the meaning become paramount and

The effect is instantaneous and
All that matters is the poem's impact.

The ear measures a poem
in the easy flow of words
within a series of
breaths.

When I hold a glass of water I can
See the absence of color and when I
Drink the water I can taste its tasteless
Quality and yet it is nourishing

Morning clarity has the same sort of
Character for me once the drowsiness
Of sleep is over as I can enjoy the
Lack of anxiety and weariness

I can see and hear the activity
Of the birds and when the cars drive by they
Reverberate and when the wind is up
The leaves are sighing and my mind isn't

Caught in resentments or worried about
The details I have no way to influence.

It's taken many decades
to appreciate the
absence of
anxiety and
agitation.

A conclusion is hanging in the air
As the apples are falling from my tree
As the sun is not as fierce as it was
And the days begin with mellow coolness

And I have lost track but it seems lately
We have so frequently begun our days
With cloudless glorious skies and mild suns
Only to be overcome by rainy

Afternoons and I must admit to an
Element of weariness about the
Endless repetitions of the seasons
As I know the days will never be more

Temperate and beautiful than now and
I really do love these quiet mornings.

Hearing crows
through my open window
punctuates
enveloping
quiet.

It's better to have a nerdy flair for
The boring details of policy to
Appreciate the glorious show of
Politics but what's absolutely key

To be a powerful politico
Is a passion for gossip and high school
Drama with a zest for secrecy and
A genius for twisting data into

Useful fables while smiling sincerely
As the creation of a comforting
Trustworthy and attractive persona
With a hint of savvy rascality

Will sway the masses of the ignorant
And capture the hearts of the gullible.

The henchmen
of democracy
are nasty but
they don't rise
to the top.

I've acquired a taste for the game of
Politics savoring verbosity
And pageantry appreciating how
Elections become the central drama

Of our culture anticipating the
Precarious balancing of power
Witnessing a truth of human nature
That audacity seizes victory

But it's also true that deception and
Power are inextricable and most
Of our politicos are selfishly
Motivated and that they are content

To exchange one pernicious policy
For an equally lousy solution.

It becomes more
difficult over the years
to tolerate the many
commonplace
lies.

I am a clever writer conniving
With co-conspirators propagating
A political agenda at odds
With the dominant ideology

Publishing a journal of opinion
With writers throughout America with
The goal of preserving liberty
Against totalitarianism

But ours is a big country with many
Divisions working at cross-purposes
And it's easier to assassinate
An opponent's character in the press

Than to explain the complexity of
Issues so we have to be circumspect.

I have the liberty
not to talk or
argue about
politics with my
family and friends.

I wheeled my container of garbage to
The curb to be picked up the next morning
And the sky was navy blue before the
Dawn and I saw a crescent moon and the

Stars glittering in luminosity
And I thought of the Chinese river and
Mountain poets alone within the wild
Country preferring isolation to

The stridency of civilization
And I wondered whether it was worth the
Loneliness to dedicate their lives to
Unhindered unfiltered experience

Listening to resonant waterfalls
Gazing at the luminous crescent moon?

The August sun
going down is a
mellow orange
and the light
on the leaves
is golden.

Last year I raked together the fallen
Apples and stooped over picking them up
And dropping the apples into lawn bags
For Waste Management to dispose of — which

Is tedious and laborious and
Lacking in dignity which prompted me
To question — why am I doing this — with
The answer being because otherwise

The neighbors will think that I'm untidy
And I realized maybe they think so
And maybe not but why should I care so
This year the apples are fermenting in

The grass providing a feast for rabbits
And squirrels and a festival of bugs.

There are only so many
apples I can eat before
they rot and apples in
lawn bags are surprisingly
heavy.

Yesterday was tainted by the threat of
An early evening storm and the vigor
Of the wind in the early afternoon
Was harsh diminishing my frolic on

My bicycle so I came home early
Anticipating intensifying
Blusters and the onset in twilight was
Overwhelming with the rain and the wind

Roaring in my cottonwood with all of
The branches flailing about as I rushed
To close my west windows while I relished
The calamitous clapping of thunder

But within five minutes it was over
And I was disappointed wanting more.

Some of the strewn cottonwood
branches on my lawn
will need to be sawed
and they won't ferment so
I need to bag them.

I share my house with Johnnie
Who is a rapacious beast
He yowls for his food
Three times in a day
Demanding another feast.

I also live with Kitcat
Who is reliably nuts
Learning from Johnnie
He yowls for his food
But then he refuses to eat.

A fly is only a fly and not worth
My noticing but Kitcat is thinking
Otherwise as he's encompassed within a
Little house and is able to see through

The windows rabbits munching grass and birds
Darting in the air but he can only
Express his energy by scrambling through
The rooms leaping into the air onto

Furniture with acrobatic aplomb
And today he was doing a dance by
Standing up on his haunches balancing
With his tail and swatting with his front paws

As an enticing and elusive object
Of joy provided meaning to his life.

I'm sure by now
he's familiar with
the taste of
flies.

I notice the way we poets employ
A straight left margin and I emphasize
Its rigidness with capital letters
And I also adhere to a form by

Utilizing ten syllables a line
And for me these devices are symbols
For the way we humans organize our
Lives separating our experience

Into minutes hours days weeks and months
And how could we do otherwise because
Segmentation is inherent in us
But I don't give a damn whether my lines

End with insignificant words because
That allows for flowing exploration.

I enjoy the tension
generated between
discipline and
spontaneity.

It's better to be grateful even in
February in Minnesota than
To be glum when the icy snow arrives
Because the sun is a welcome blessing

Throughout the year with a rainbow spectrum
Of appearances and even on a
Cloudy day in winter the sun lights the
Earth while we could be set within the blaze

Of the perpetually drifting sands
Of the Sahara without rivers and
Trees where the sun is a menace rising
Over the horizon broiling every

Grain of sand compelling every thought to
Endurance — baking every molecule.

The sun in Minnesota
is mild enough
to raise a garden
paradise.

Driving around town amidst the golden
Light of August I am seeing many
Kinds of riding lawnmowers of a sort
That specializes in taking care of

Swaths of grass between offices or on
A golf course and if I were so employed
I'd prefer the type in which the rider
Is standing rather than sitting because

Over every rise and hollow would be
The sensation of riding the swells and
Troughs of the fluctuating ocean and
I'd like to be rising and falling and

Flexing my knees pirouetting around
Trees and manhandling those swirling blades.

I wouldn't have to
think about anything
other than delusions
of grandeur.

I have a comforting memory of
Camping with my family when I was
A child of watching the wind making the
Leaves of a single slender poplar tree

Sigh as I was impacted by the grace
Of the turning leaves and of the swaying
Of the tree as something inside of me
Responded saying here is peace and this

Is beautiful and there really is no
Reason to be afraid or upset with
The chaotic appearances of things
Because underneath it all there is a

Gentleness and a harmony that the
Mind of a quiet child can recognize.

Now and then
without conscious effort
the image of the poplar
in the wind
reemerges.

I know Doug from the gym and he urged me
To ditch the stationary bike and spend
My saved-up money on a genuine
Road bicycle and so this summer I

Did and we aren't conniving to meet but
It's happening that on the trails we are
Coming across each other and he's the
Veteran and there was a day he left

Me behind but I'm stubborn and I use
The method of persistency and we've
Taken to racing up the hill into
Houlton rising off our seats to sprint to

The top and he usually wins but
Yesterday I managed to edge him out.

We are a couple
of roving sports
bypassing
dilettantes and
sluggards.

I saw a slender tree in the wind with
Its leaves turning and sighing with the breeze
When I was young enough not to have a
Developed vocabulary so I

Didn't know it was a poplar tree and
Couldn't have said why it was peaceful and
Beautiful but that momentary sight
Of a single tree swaying in a breeze

Has grown deep roots within me as the tree
Was there that day to give me and only
Me a vision embedding hints inside
Of me that even though there is such

Awful striving in life I can find a
Way to drop the stress and be full of peace.

To a child's eyes
visions come
unfiltered by
experience.

Yesterday was a good day to be shown
That no matter how good I think I am
Another cyclist will probably come
From behind and pass me by as happened

On the arduous hill to Houlton but
Smelling the cow manure at the top
Flying downward over the Crossing Bridge
To the long decline into Stillwater

Savoring the liberation of speed
Seeing the sunflowers and wildflowers
Hearing the crickets from within the grass
Watching afternoon shadows lengthen was

Worth my pedaling the circuit over
And over again until my crotch hurt.

The pinnacle
of summer
is worthy of
exhaustion
mixed with
satisfaction.

I bicycle over two bridges and
Around a river valley while at the
Same time the earth is rotating on its
Axis and orbiting the sun of our

Solar system and our solar system
Is not idle but is orbiting a
Spiraling galaxy that we call the
Milky Way and the Milky Way isn't

Idle either as it's moving away
From whatever happened that we call the
Big Bang however long ago that was
And where the Milky Way is going is

Hard to say except that it's expanding
Amidst trillions of other galaxies.

So I'm a speck
on a bicycle
cycling within cycles
pedaling who knows
where?

During the t-shirt and short pants days of
Summer it's difficult to imagine
The absence of the leaves even though I've
Seen the bare branches of winter for year

After year and I've heard the lamenting
Wind in the naked trees — and even on
The coldest overcast February
Morning it's tricky to imagine the

Absence of the sun because then the day
Would be in total darkness and the cold
Would be even colder — and it's even
Trickier to imagine the absence

Of the earth because there would be nowhere
To stand without the slightest gust of wind.

Perhaps it's impossible
but try to imagine
the absence of everything
which is the emptiness
from which we come.

There's a corner of the windowsill where
I can see the gossamer threads of a
Spider's web but I am usually
Cogitating about writing something

And seeing clouds and leaves is expansive
But gazing at the corner is boring
And it takes effort to rise from my chair
To get a paper towel and clean it up

But the other day I actually
Saw a delicate and spindly spider
Spinning another thread and I thought how
Diligent and admirable and how

Worthy of my attention and I can
See him now hanging quite motionless.

Later I will curl
fifty-pound dumbbells
twenty-five times in a row
but I'll probably leave
the spider alone.

It would be tricky to see because it
Moves about at night and it resembles
An oversized rat with an extremely
Elongated nose culminating with

What looks like a pig's snout that really is
An excellent sniffer and maybe its
Most salient attribute is its most
Adroit and lengthy tongue capable of

Catching its skittering prey and I do
Puzzle over how a creature with such
Equipment could manage to swallow but
Somehow it does and it trots around on

Four powerful legs with sharp claws that are
Superb for defense and for burrowing.

Besides being one of the
first words appearing in the
dictionary it's odd
because who could invent
the name — aardvark?

Why anyone would want to do such a
Thing that goes against every instinct is
Truly beyond me as I discovered
Last year that such mild activity as

Swinging my partner in a line dance would
Make me dizzy surpassing the point of
Nausea but to tether one's foot to
A cord and jump from the safety of a

Bridge and plunge headlong through a depth only
To be stopped and jerked upward again by
A bungee cord as the jumper must be
An adrenaline junkie addled with

Insanity without a sense of grace
Willing to impersonate a yo-yo.

To be bag of bones
and innards depending
on the elasticity of
any random cord
is bonkers.

Summer is the season for the city
To excavate the streets upgrading the
Concrete drainage system and they are not
Replacing the entire street but they

Are doing patch work and complicating
An already hodgepodge surface that makes
Me maneuver down a side street a block
Beside my usual route exploring

Houses and yards I've never seen after
Living in Stillwater for decades and
I could be driving about in any
Town USA and it's remarkable

To recognize how much like a mouse in
A comfortable maze that I've become.

The city has an army
of trucks and treaded
vehicles with different
kinds of steel shovels
and pulverizing tools.

The city snowplow has its opposite
Once the weather starts to rain again and
The street sweeper is the oddest-looking
Vehicle being boxy in the front

And tapering to a point with only
One double wheel behind and the purpose
Of the contraption is to clear the street
Of the accumulated grit and bits

Of glass and of the twigs and leaves that are
Constantly present because nobody
Else but the city is assuming the
Responsibility and without the

Periodic operation of the
Sweeper we'd all be living in a dump.

Angled disks on both sides
of the city sweeper
swirl bristles around
and around making
life tolerable.

At the garden section of Home Depot
Twenty years ago I bought two apple
Trees without any knowledge about the
Variety of types and presently

My choices are bearing fruit as one of
Them is generating yellow and soft
Apples at the end of July but the
Other is providing crisper red and

Yellow apples ripening finally
In September and I'm happy with the
Yellow apples because they are tasty
But the later red and yellow ones are

Bitter and hard and maybe the rabbits
And squirrels can digest them but not me.

Like politicians
the nature of the
apple tree is
revealed
eventually.

The bitter and hard apples
take longer to become
mush and dissolve into
the earth but it does
happen.

— Tekkan